I Ain't Down Yet

The Autobiography of My Little Margie

by

Gale Storm

with
BILL LIBBY

THE BOBBS-MERRILL COMPANY, INC.
Indianapolis/New York

Published by The Bobbs-Merrill Company, Inc.
Indianapolis   New York

Library of Congress Cataloging in Publication Data

Storm, Gale, 1922–
  "I ain't down yet."
  1. Storm, Gale, 1922–.   2. Actors—
United States—Biography.   3. Christian
biography—United States.   I. Libby, Bill.
II. Title.   III. Title: My little Margie.
PN2287.S76A34   791.45′028′0924   [B] 81-66312
ISBN 0-672-52684-0   AACR2

Designed by Jacques Chazaud
Manufactured in the United States of America

First printing

To my husband,
Whom I love so fiercely and so passionately
that he must wish for a dull moment at times.

The authors wish to thank Lee Bonnell for his help with this book.

Also, Herb Pratt, Mike Dunn, Thom Schneidt and Jack Fahey of Raleigh Hills Hospital and its parent company, Advanced Health Systems. And a very special thanks to Thad A. Eckman.

And Jackie Sommers and Mary Kraaft, Allyson Adler and Laurie Libby, and Bill Adler.

The authors also wish to thank Meredith Willson for his gracious permission to use the title of his composition, "I Ain't Down Yet," as the title of this book.

I Ain't Down Yet

(From the musical play *The Unsinkable Molly Brown*, sung by Molly as her brothers push her down.)

I ain't down yet,
I ain't down yet,
I ain't down yet . . . .
Sure, I'm tuckered
And I might give out,
But I won't give in. . . .
How can anybody say
That I'm down?
Look, I'm thinking,
I'm thinking very hard
How to break through. . . .
Maybe here, maybe there,
Maybe nowhere,
But there'll come a time!
'Cause nothing nor nobody wants me down
Like I wants me up,
Up where the people are;
Up where the talkin' is;
Up where the joke's goin' on!

Now, looky here,
I am important to me.
I ain't no bottom to no pile.
I mean much more to me
Than I mean to anybody
I ever knew . . .
Certainly more than any
Siwash, yazzyhammers like you guys!
Go ahead, break my arm. . . .
Me say uncle? Hah!
J'ever try steppin' on a piss-ant?
Well, there's one now . . .
Jump him, stomp him!
You thinkin' you got him,
You thinkin' he's quit?
Well, he don't think so!
There he goes!
And you can be positive sure
I'm as good as any piss-ant you ever saw!
Oh, I hate that word 'down,'
But I love that word 'up'!
'Cause up means hope,
And that's just what I got . . .
Hope!

Foreword

Gale Storm is as bubbly as "My Little Margie," the character she was known for on television. She comes to the door of her suburban home singing. She walks through the house singing. When she is not singing, she is humming. Or talking. She is one terrific talker.

Most of the interviews for this book were done in her home. I'd ask her a question and get ten different answers. She'd rattle on, stopping a story in the middle, jumping to another, then jumping back. If her husband, Lee, came in, he'd straighten out her stories. Then she'd straighten out his.

The phone would keep ringing and she'd keep saying, "Darn!" tell me to turn my tape recorder off for a while, jump up to answer the phone, and return to try to figure out where she had been when we'd left off. She was always running off to do something somewhere.

She'd excuse herself to go upstairs, then holler down, "I have something to show you," *then* holler down, "But not yet because I'm still looking for it." Then she'd start back downstairs saying, "I have something I want you to read. I'll explain all the big words to you."

I came to see that she is a uniquely witty lady who has something funny to say about everything. When funny things pop into her head they pop right out of her mouth. Although she has been through several kinds of hell, she doesn't take herself or her life too seriously.

It is clear she and her husband have deep feelings for each other;

she pokes fun at their relationship. He is more serious, but loves to laugh with her. They are remarkably good together.

It was difficult to get her sense of humor on paper. She is continually whooping with laughter. When she declares that she has become "a woman of the cloth," she explodes with laughter. She means that she is doing good deeds, but only *possibly* should be canonized for them. Take whatever she says with a grain of salt. Or pepper.

My job was to let her have her say. I have told her story in her own words—though I did have to move them around a little bit to get them into some sort of sequence. I wound up with three times as many pages of transcript from my recording sessions with her as I have gleaned from the most articulate of my other subjects.

But, as she rattled on, I came to realize that she could see beneath the surface of the actualities of her life as few subjects whom I've ever dealt with can. She has insights into the human spirit, and she digs as deeply as anyone could. She is a very bright lady. Too, she has an honesty that is rare. She kept going back to some subject to be sure she had set it straight. Not to make herself look better, but to show herself as she really had been or is. If she was going to tell her story, she was going to tell it true.

She tells the bad as well as the good. She reveals the lows as well as the highs. She is completely candid, not only about her alcoholism, but about her life with her husband and children, their troubles, their religion, sex, money, everything.

Talking of the people she has worked with, many of them prominent, she tells us not only about the wonderful ones but also about those who seemed to her less than wonderful. Yet she has little malice in her; she prefers a positive attitude toward life.

She tells it all as it was, and is.

She has not aged. She is beautiful.

I found her to be a great, gutsy gal, and I came to love her. I hope you will, too.

B. L.
Westminster, California
1981

Alcoholism is a disease . . . just as deadly as cancer. But you don't hear anyone say to a victim of cancer, "Use your willpower." Or, "You're too intelligent to keep drinking when you can see what it's doing to you."

I know, because my mind became a battlefield filled with those phrases until my burden of guilt, shame, and disgust replaced my self-respect, self-esteem, and sense of worth. It seemed that no matter how hard I tried, no matter how many different methods I went through, I'd end up right back where I started.

Then a friend told my husband and me about Raleigh Hills Hospitals for alcoholism. Their medical treatment is unlike any I had tried. For me, and for thousands of others, it works!

I thank God for the miracle Raleigh Hills has made in my life. It can do the same for you or someone you care about.

Gale Storm TV commercial, early 1980

1

I ain't down yet." I've played *The Unsinkable Molly Brown* on stage many times, and have sort of adopted the opening song as my own theme for life. It is talked as much as it is sung, and it sort of typifies my story. I sing it sometimes when I'm moody or depressed. To myself. "I ain't down yet . . . Oh, I hate that word 'down' but I love that word 'up' . . . 'Cause up means hope . . . "

I have hope now. A few years ago I didn't. I was drinking too much. It's hard for an alcoholic to admit it. Even to himself, or herself. I don't think many others knew it.

I was "My Little Margie." Bright as a button. Cutest thing going. Sweet and innocent; pure as the driven snow. From my movie days I had the reputation of a family lady, a religious woman. Most of the fan magazine stories about me were called things like "Family Comes First for Gale" or "Her Religion Rates Tops."

My family *did* come first with me. My husband, Lee Bonnell, and our four children were the most important things in my life. They still are. My religion was always an important part of my life; we went to church every Sunday; I taught Sunday School; I believed.

Few would expect any extremes of me, much less that I'd drink too much. But I did—so much that I'm lucky I didn't lose my husband and children. I didn't lose faith in God, nor did I wonder why He was doing this to me. I wondered why *I* was doing this to me.

I don't know why I started drinking. Most people assume that

1

alcoholics are unhappy people. And maybe they are. They certainly are by the time they have become alcoholics. In the beginning maybe most of them start to drink to excess because they feel they are unlucky in love or life, because they feel they've failed in one way or another and want to forget their failures, and they sink into some drunken, drugged state to hide from life.

That certainly wasn't true for me. My marriage of more than thirty years was as sound as ever. My husband was well established in his own profession. I was doing well in mine. My career wasn't at its peak, but I was working in dinner theater across the country.

Success never meant all that much to me, but I was fortunate enough to have my fair share of it. I was an actress and a star of "B" movies in the 1940s. I was Gale Storm and the fan magazines were full of stories about me.

Ironically, television, not movies, gave me my real prominence, with "My Little Margie" in the early 1950s and "Oh! Susanna" in the late 1950s. Both were big hits, often rated in the top ten. "Oh! Susanna" was a sort of forerunner of "The Love Boat."

I spent ten years or so, not counting reruns, on prime time TV. I made albums and single records that were rated in the top ten. I played Las Vegas. I was a guest on all the top television shows. It was fun for me and I enjoyed it. I took it in stride. I love performing. But it didn't alter my life a great deal.

My TV and record career began to fade, but I kept active starring in stage plays all across the country. I had made a lot of money; I was still doing well. My husband's income was more than sufficient. Our kids were doing well. We had a nice home, a good life. We had our problems—who doesn't? But there were none we couldn't or didn't deal with. I started to drink in the early 1960s, however, and I started to drink too much in the early 1970s.

Let's backtrack: I didn't have a drink of alcohol of any kind until I was twenty-one. I was born Josephine Owaissa Cottle in Texas, which was then a dry state. I was reared by my mother, who didn't drink, and I didn't grow up around people who drank. I was told drinking did you no good, so I disapproved of it.

My husband, Lee, a college man, drank, but not often and not much. When he did, he got a glare from me. He was sophisticated. He liked a drink, but he never needed one. That's the difference.

I Ain't Down Yet

The first time I drank, I got sick. It was at a Christmas party in our neighborhood. A friend insisted I take a drink. I didn't have to, of course, but everyone else was drinking, and I didn't want to be a spoilsport.

It tasted terrific. Ah-ha! I was surprised to find that I really liked it. In fact, it tasted so good I didn't think it could be a hard drink. (It was only Southern Comfort—100 proof.) I thought I handled it and the few that followed perfectly well. Until I got up to go . . . and fell on my face.

Lee had to carry me home. I was sick all night and throughout the next day. After I threw up what I had in my stomach, the dry heaves went on and on. I didn't have another drink for almost ten years.

By then, I didn't disapprove of drinking. We went to Hollywood parties and I got used to being around drinking. It was difficult *not* to drink. People made it that way: you know, "Are you sure you won't have a drink? Just one little one?"

I stood around for years holding a Coke or a 7-Up or orange juice in a glass in my hand so people wouldn't pester me: I acted as if I had a drink in my hand. I was a good little actress.

I don't really know when I started to drink. I really don't. It just happened. Somewhere along the way I took one. And then another. It happened to be vodka. I happened to like it. So I started to take vodka drinks at parties. Soon I didn't have to hold a Coke or a 7-Up.

I was strictly a social drinker, or thought I was. For many years, I had just a drink or two at parties. I don't know when it started to be more than that. Probably in the early 1970s, I just started to drink more and more.

I think it began with a drink before dinner. A little wine. Then a harder drink. Maybe a vodka martini. Then a drink after dinner. Very civilized. Then a drink before lunch. Even more civilized. Then a drink after lunch. Or when I came home from work—or Lee came home from work. Everyone's entitled to relax with a drink after work, right?

Then I found myself waking up in the middle of the night needing a drink. I'd sneak downstairs and have a drink or two of vodka—straight. Then I found myself needing a drink when I woke up in the morning. So I had a drink before breakfast. And lunch. And dinner. It just got away from me. Before I knew it, I was drinking all the time.

3

We had an unusual house, U-shaped and very deep. Before long, I didn't want to be too far from a drink. So I stashed bottles at each end. No matter where I was in the house I was always at least halfway to a drink.

Lee might call me to see if he could pick up something I needed on his way home from the office. I'd make up a couple of things and then say, "Oh, yes, I think we're out of vodka. Maybe you could pick up a bottle." He'd say, "What kind?" and I'd say, "It doesn't matter. Maybe Smirnoff's."

It did matter and it didn't matter. If I had to, I'd drink any kind. But I thought Smirnoff's was the best. And I knew what I wanted: blue label, 100 proof. Sometimes when I felt saintly I'd buy the silver label, which was only 90 proof. He'd bring home the regular label, which was only 84 proof. I knew all the labels. I had my drinking down to a science. I bought a bottle every time I was at the market or near a liquor store, but I still had Lee bring home a bottle when I could. I only felt safe when I knew I had enough in reserve.

Of course Lee started to see that I was drinking too much. At first he'd just give me a look—a "Haven't-you-had-enough?" look. Then he started to say, "Don't you think you've had enough?" I'd ignore him. Or I might say, "Oh, I'm fine. Just one more maybe." Or maybe I wouldn't take that one drink in front of him—I'd go off and sneak one. And at first he didn't realize how much I was drinking. He didn't think I was an alcoholic or anything like that.

But after a while he started to check the bottles at home. He'd sneak a look. Or pour himself a drink so he could sneak a look. He didn't think I knew, but I did. We drinkers are shrewd. I started to drink just a little out of the bottle that was in sight so that when he checked it, it wasn't too bad. I had other bottles I could drink from. I had them hidden all over the house. When we moved to another house, the moving men found bottles I'd hidden and forgotten.

I was a very careful drinker. I never drank before an interview. Or during one, like at lunch, maybe. Perhaps one, nursing it. I didn't want to be obvious. I never drank before a show. I had too much respect for my profession and my fellow actors for that. And I had enough sense to know I could destroy my career. So I was sober for all my performances. And that probably bought me a few years of drinking before it became a problem for me. And it wasn't too hard. It would have been if I hadn't known I could go home later and drink all I wanted to.

I fortified myself with a few drinks before going to parties so I wouldn't feel the need to drink too much in public. Offered a drink, I'd say, "I would like a double vodka martini, straight up, with a twist of lemon, very, very dry, cha-cha-cha." The twist of lemon was a nice touch—an olive took up too much room. So did ice. I never ordered drinks with ice. And I'd stroll to the other side of the room so I could have another drink. Whatever drink I had always was "my first." But I was careful never to have too many in public. Alcoholics are cunning.

I don't think anyone outside my family realized how much I was drinking, at least not for a long time. There are a lot of myths about alcoholics, and we'll get into most of them later. An alcoholic can exercise willpower and he can be careful. He doesn't have to drink all the time—many can quit. For days, weeks, maybe months. But an alcoholic who doesn't know he *is* one will start again.

There are many different definitions of an alcoholic. He doesn't have to drink at work and he doesn't have to drink at home. Maybe he does these things, but he can be an alcoholic without doing them. He can say, as so many do, "I never drink before five," or "I only drink on weekends," and he can be telling the truth, but he still can be an alcoholic.

He doesn't have to be a he. He can be a she, as I am. There may not be as many women alcoholics as men alcoholics, but there are more than most people realize. That's because women hide it more. Drinking is supposed to be a macho game. Men are more likely to go into bars alone, "to be with the boys." Men laugh about getting drunk. We laugh with them. Usually. No one laughs at a drunken woman. I don't know why. So, women hide drinking more than men do.

I don't know when I actually became an alcoholic. Certainly not for a long while. I drank a lot for a long time—five or six years—but I thought I could handle it. I was careful. I didn't drink too much in public. I was never a falling-down drunk. I watched where I walked. I never embarrassed myself. It's funny, but I was better coordinated when I was drinking than I am today. Now, if I trip anywhere, over anything, I laugh about it, saying, "I never did that when I was drinking." Anyone can trip, but when you're drinking it's always blamed on your being drunk. It's all right for me to trip now.

I made light of my drinking. I seldom spilled a drop, but if I did, I smiled ever so sweetly and said, "I don't like to drink the stuff; I wear it." In the end, I was getting a quart of vodka into me a day without wearing any of it. For a long time it didn't show. I figured I could handle it. I had a hollow leg. I could drink more and more without feeling it. I didn't realize that I had to drink more and more to satisfy my needs. My body was demanding more and more, which is why I was waking up with the need for a drink.

Because I controlled when and where I drank, I thought I could stop whenever I wanted. I didn't put it to a test; I didn't dare. The fact was that I could put off having a drink when it would show because I knew I could drink when I was alone. At the end of the day or night, at home or in a hotel on the road, I could drink. I was a closet drinker, and I guarantee you there were bottles in the closet. I was proud of my ability to drink without getting drunk.

My mind demanded another drink because my body needed it. I was hooked on alcohol as surely as a narcotics addict is hooked on heroin or cocaine. My husband saw it long before I did. And our youngest child, our daughter, saw it but didn't know what to do about it. The other children were grown and gone. Susie started leaving around pamphlets from Alcoholics Anonymous. I'd throw them out; they made me mad. I drank, but I wasn't an alcoholic. I was so self-righteous!

It was hard for Lee to lecture me. He's a very sweet man who really loves me. He would put up with anything for me. He didn't lose his temper or threaten me or anything like that. He tried to talk to me. I wouldn't listen. For a while I'd argue with him. When I ran out of arguments, I stopped answering him. Maybe I'd say, "I don't want to talk about it," but that's all I'd ever say. If he kept talking about it, I'd get angry and storm out of the room. When you're wrong about something and won't admit it, you get away from it; you run away from it. You ignore it in the hope that it will go away.

I love Lee. But I hated it when he talked about my drinking. I became very antagonistic toward him, critical of him in any way I could be because he had become critical of me. You try to cut others down to your size. You become so cunning, consumed with the desire to do whatever you have to do to make it possible for you to continue drinking. Lee suffered so much. Your family suffers too, because they care and can't do anything to help you.

I let Lee plan our lives. He got used to making all the decisions. Many people enjoy that sort of power. In a way they don't want their alcoholics to change, because then *they* stay in charge. It makes them feel that they are the strong ones. Whether they'll admit it to themselves or not, they like the feeling. Lee isn't like that; nonetheless, it was hard for him later when I got sober and demanded the right to share in our life.

For a long time, I had surrendered my status as an equal partner in our life. Lee was sort of my manager anyway, and he always made the decisions as to what jobs I took or which shows I did. I wanted him to. All I cared about was protecting my privacy, being able to go on with my drinking. I was half a person. Less than that. I was an alcoholic. Hard to believe: My Little Margie and Susanna added up to one alcoholic!

You'd think I could have seen myself, wouldn't you? But I wouldn't look. I had become an alcoholic, and in my heart I think I knew it; but in my mind I wouldn't admit it. I didn't know it until I saw it: in the bathroom mirror. All of a sudden my drinking showed. In six months my weight had shot way up; I don't know how far—I wouldn't weigh myself. But, incredibly, in six short months, I got fat; even my face got fat. I ran the hot water in the shower so the mirror would steam up and I couldn't see myself when I got out.

Here I was, jeopardizing my career and my marriage. I wasn't working very much.

It was not the most important thing, but the straw that broke the camel's back might have been vanity. I had always been told I was a pretty girl. I wasn't vain about it but I knew it and I liked it. I know it helped me get into plays in school. It helped me get into the movies. I was pretty; I did not think I was beautiful. There were greater beauties; I envied them. I was cute. Sometimes I hated it. Being forever young. When you're young, you want to be older. I looked like a nice girl. I was a nice girl. But sometimes you want people to think of you as a temptress. I was always the girl next door. Necking on the living room couch, maybe, but never in the bedroom.

Now here, all those years later, was vanity taking over. In six short

7

months or so I started to look terrible. My face got rounder than ever. People used to marvel about how I kept my trim little figure and never put on weight. I stayed thin.

Suddenly I was fat. Look, I'm short—five feet four. And I never weighed more than a hundred and four to a hundred and eight. There I was, getting wider. I was ashamed to shop in my favorite places. I went where no one knew me. I bought dresses that I hoped would hide my weight. But there was no hiding it. I started to feel lousy, too. I wasn't eating much. I was gaining weight because I was drinking. Too much. And for too long.

Lee finally talked me into going to a doctor. I had told this man before that I was a social drinker, but this time I couldn't say that; I couldn't get away with it. His tests showed that my liver had become enlarged to three or four times its normal size. I looked as though I were six months pregnant. The doctor's tests showed that much of my body was affected. His tests proved that I was drinking myself to death. I didn't like him for telling me that. But by then I had to face it.

I was an alcoholic. I could no longer hide it. I was told I had to stop drinking, but I knew I couldn't. I had tried and I couldn't. I had to have a drink. I hated myself for it. I was sick of myself. I was no good and I knew it. Lee tried to help, but he couldn't.

I had to have help. Lee saw it, and even I could see it. But where would we *get* help? We had tried everything. We tried counseling, we tried Alcoholics Anonymous, we tried doctors, we tried hospitals, we even tried a psychiatric ward.

For a long time nothing worked; there was no help for me. How could this be happening to me? Lee asked me to pray with him. Not for forgiveness; it never occurred to me that God wouldn't forgive me. But for help. It hurt me to pray, but Lee wanted me to. He was so frustrated by his inability to help me that I had to help *him*.

Every morning, when we woke up and dressed, before we did anything else, we went into the kitchen and sat down and held hands and prayed to God for help. Lee prayed. I didn't. I prayed desperately at first, but when my prayers weren't answered, I stopped. I didn't want to ask anything for myself. Lee was asking for me, and I felt unworthy. I didn't want to ask God to forgive me, because I couldn't forgive myself. So I'd sit there, head bowed, holding hands with my husband, knowing he was praying for me, wanting to pray for myself but unable to do it, feeling as though I were out of touch with the world, a stranger to my husband, an outcast from life who could not be helped. It was a terrible, terrifying time.

It's strange, but my life had been beautiful. It had been a story out of a book. Josephine Cottle didn't have a lot back in Texas, but she won a national radio contest and a screen contract in Hollywood and a new name. And she married the man who won the male half of that contest. And had been married to him for thirty years. And had had four fine children with him. I had been a star in movies and on television, on stage and in recording studios. I didn't need anything. There were no sudden, dramatic developments in my life; there was no divorce, no death. I was the star of my own cornball "B" movie, and suddenly it turned into a horror story. Here is that story. The Josephine Cottle story.

2

My most vivid memory of my childhood is of my mother bending over a sewing machine. She always seemed to be there. For hours and hours, night after night. For a long time that was how she supported her family of five. She made and mended clothes for us. And she took in sewing for others. For most of my growing-up years, we had little.

I was born Josephine Owaissa Cottle on the fifth of April, 1922. "Owaissa" means "bluebird" in Indian. I don't know what tribe. I don't *think* I have any Indian blood in me.

My mother remembered coming from Virginia to Texas in a covered wagon when she was a little girl. My father's family came to Texas even earlier. One of them was supposedly a hero at the Alamo.

The only grandparent I remember—my paternal grandfather— used to take me on his knee and tell me stories about how his people came to Texas in those wagons. They were pioneers; his people were among the earliest settlers in the state.

For a long time I thought everyone studied Texas history in school. Texas is very important to Texans. But I don't feel like a Texan anymore. I moved away a long time ago. And I haven't been back many times lately.

My grandfather died many years ago. My father, W. W. Cottle—William Walter Cottle—died when I was thirteen months old. He was a potter. According to my mother, he was perfection.

She put on his tombstone: "He was too good for earth. . . . God called him home."

I was the fifth of five children. I had two older sisters and two older brothers.

My sisters have both died. My sister Lois was thirteen years older than I and died in the late 1970s. She married a man named Stelle, then he died, and she married a man named Howard Milligan. She had a son and daughter by her first husband. My sister Marjorie, seven years older than I, died in the early 1970s. She married Chester Divine and they adopted a daughter, Sharon.

My oldest brother, Wilbur, is eleven years older than I. He went to work for the Humble Oil Company when he was fourteen or fifteen years old and took an early retirement when he was sixty. He and his wife have a son, Will, and an adopted daughter, Shirley, and live in Elgin, Texas.

The younger of my brothers, Joel Braxton—known as "Brack"—is five years older than I am. He's a pilot and head of maintenance for the Beechcraft Airplane Company at Van Nuys airport. He and his wife have a son, Joel, and two daughters, Geraldine and Joan. They live in Saugus, in the San Fernando Valley.

The first-, third-, and fifth-born in my family were girls. The second- and fourth-born were boys. I came along after a five-year break, like an accident. I was always "Baby Jo."

I was born in Bloomington, Texas, but my parents moved soon afterward and I've never been back. We moved to McDade, but then we moved again right away, and I don't remember much about McDade. I was two or three when we settled in Houston, and that is the Texas I remember.

We stayed in Houston until I left Texas, but we kept moving from house to house. Most of the houses were small, many of them not really houses, as I remember. They were more like additions to houses, and we rented them. The house numbers usually had a half or a quarter after them, as if they were afterthoughts. We generally moved to a cheaper place because we couldn't afford the one we had.

My mother, Minnie Corina—her real middle name was Greenhaw, but she didn't like it and changed it—opened a millinery shop, making hats, and then branched out to dresses. The shop failed in McDade, and when we moved to Houston, she earned her living as a seamstress. She had regular customers.

It must have been hard on her, supporting five children on that sort of work. Every night, late, she was leaning over that sewing machine. And of course she cooked for us, and kept the house clean. She kept us in line—she was strict. She used a switch on us, a twig with the leaves pulled off. She always said, "Don't dispute my word," and I never did.

Our religion was important to her. It became important to me. We went to St. John's Methodist Church in Houston. Mother was sewing, even on Sunday mornings, so sometimes she couldn't go, but she always saw to it that we went. I went to church and to Sunday School. I liked it. I liked church and learning about God. I loved God; I didn't fear Him.

When I was only ten years old I made my own decision to be baptized—sprinkled, when you're a Methodist. The spiritual side of my life was and is as important as any other side. I try to guide my life by God's laws.

We didn't have a lot when I was growing up, but I always gave thanks to God for what I had. I was taught not to pray to Him just for those things I wanted, the way any child wants things. Mom saw to it that we didn't lack the important things. I always knew the difference between things we needed to have and things we wanted to have.

Mother made all our clothes. She was clever; she could take a piece of cloth and make me a dress or a skating costume, or one for a school play. But when I wanted to be in the Girl Scouts or something like a Booster Club in school which called for an official costume, I just accepted the fact that I couldn't have it. If she couldn't make it, we couldn't afford it.

Those were depression days. We were poor, and we didn't have many luxuries, but I was happy. We had a radio I listened to all the time. And sometimes we went to the movies. When I started to date, our social life was centered on dances. I didn't think I was missing out on a lot.

I guess because I was the baby, the last born, the one most at home, I was close to my mother. The year I started to go out, my mother would always encourage me, but several hours before time for me to leave she'd begin with, "Well, I'll be alone tonight. . . .

But you go on . . . you go have a good time. . . . I do get lonely, you know . . . home all alone. . . . But I want my children to have a good time. . . . No one can say I don't want my children to have a good time."

I'd say, "Mother, you make me feel awful . . ." and she'd say, "I don't want you to feel awful. . . ." But of course she did. I'd offer to stay home, and she'd say, "Oh, no, dear, you go and have a good time. I'll be all right. I'll keep busy. It's just so hard to be alone on a Saturday night." She'd drive me to tears of frustration, but I caught on eventually that it was a game with her. She really was alone a lot. And sometimes I would stay home with her. But most of the time I went out, just as all the other kids did. Feeling guilty, of course. Mothers are marvels at making kids feel guilty.

Eventually she remarried. When I was about thirteen or fourteen. A man named Mr. Skadden. I don't remember his first name, which shows you how close we were. Mother was only married to him for eight to ten years; I don't even remember what he did for a living.

He wasn't a bad person, but he wasn't an important part of my life. In a way, he took my mother away from me, although we moved in with him into a big house. I was as possessive of her as she was of me, I guess. I resented him a little. He came along too late to be a father to me. I'd been so young when I lost my father that I didn't know what it was like to *have* one.

Mr. Skadden had a daughter who was about my age and two older sons. They told me how marvelous it was going to be to have a sister my age, but it wasn't. Her name was Helen and she was very unlike me. She was a tomboy and I wasn't. I was pretty and she wasn't. I was popular and she wasn't, and she resented it. I tried to get her dates and make it up to her, but she didn't want to be friends with me. Her father gave her money and things and never gave me anything. He was never a father to me, and she was never a sister to me.

I was always an active child. I was one of the best skaters at the Polar Palace, and one of the best dancers anywhere. I was always in the school plays and musicals. I went to Henry Wadsworth Longfellow Elementary School, Albert Sydney Johnson Junior High School and San Jacinto High School—and I was one of the most popular students at any of them. I think it is important to say this so

13

you know what sort of life I had before the bottle. My early life was great. I wasn't touched by hard times.

I did well with my studies, skipping a couple of grades along the way. So I was a year or two younger than most of the kids in my class after a while, and I started to date early.

A lot of boys asked me for dates, but it bothered me when certain ones didn't ask. It's the ones you don't have that you always want. So I decided there had to be a way to get someone you especially wanted interested in you.

This was my way, and it was all mine. Please don't tell anyone. But it can change your life.

There was this one boy who never paid any attention to me and it was driving me mad. He was a football star at Johnson Junior High. His name was Dick Van Orden, and now he will be forever famous. The only time I saw him was in the hallways between classes, so that was when I had to attract him.

I tried it out on other boys first to perfect it, then gave it the big test with him. The secret was eye contact. Whenever I saw him I would fix my gaze on him and stare. I'd keep my expression pleasant. I didn't smile at him or frown. I didn't bat my eyes at him or wink at him. I just simply *looked* at him, as pleasantly as possible. I practiced until I could put just a hint of admiration into my look. Not a lot; just enough so he was aware that I felt he was special.

I never went up to him. I never volunteered a word. If he nodded to me, I nodded back. If he said "Hi," I said "Hi." And he started to nod to me and say "Hi." He began to notice me, and that took care of the first part of my plan. He had started to anticipate my looking at him, to bask in that hint of admiration in my gaze. Everybody likes to be noticed and admired. He was ripe for the picking.

So then I started *not* to look at him. Not as though I were angry with him or anything. Just as though I no longer noticed him. Just as I'd pass him, I'd notice someone somewhere else and shift my gaze. After a while I knew I was getting to him. He'd start to nod or say "Hi" and I'd be past him. I could see he had become accustomed to being someone special in my eyes, and it bothered him that suddenly he wasn't.

So after there was nothing for Dick to do but ask me for a date, I went out with him a few times. Then I went out with someone else, and someone else after that. A lot of them were nice, and I dated them all. I didn't have a lot of steadies. We went skating or swimming or dancing, we went to the movies, we necked in parked cars; but we didn't do much more than that. In the late 1930s I was younger than the others. But whenever I wanted a date with someone who wasn't asking me for one, I used my eye-contact technique and it never failed.

Maybe it wouldn't have worked so well if I had been homely; but almost everything worked for me in those days. I was a good actress, even then.

I played lead after lead in plays and musicals as I went along in school. From the time I was a little kid, when we put together neighborhood shows, I sang and danced. I had no training. We couldn't afford any kind of lessons. But I went on—and wished. There were wishes that weren't granted. I went on.

I lost the lead in one play, but I played another part, and the next year I had the lead. I sang and danced and won the declamation contest and, with it, the American Legion Award. I have a letter written to me by Rona Collier, one of my teachers, when I graduated: "Dearest Josephine, I can't realize that today was your last day at Johnson. No one will miss you as much as I, but you will be greatly missed by the entire school. We've learned to call on you on important occasions, and you've always come smiling through, to the great credit of yourself and your school.

"A great honor was conferred on you this week, my dear. As you go into senior high school you must carry with you the same ideals and always have the courage to hold to them. That sweet smile is going to bring a lot of happiness to this old world."

She later taught me at San Jacinto High. She and a Miss Oatman were really great influences on me. I was supersensitive. I was so hurt when leads were taken away from me that I worried about hurting those I took leads from later on. I dreaded losing leads but I had to gather up my courage to try out for them. Then it took all my courage to wait for my fate. When the "Gateway to Hollywood" contest came to town, both Miss Collier and Miss Oatman insisted I enter. I told them I was scared. They said I had to have courage. But I was only seventeen years old, just a baby. I wasn't even finished with my senior year in high school.

I never had a single thought that the movies could happen. I had no idea what I was going to do with my life, but I never thought of going to Hollywood. Years later, those two teachers were brought out to be with me on one of Ralph Edwards' "This Is Your Life" television shows. This was my life. Baby Jo was about to grow up.

3

I n the 1930s, there was no television. Radio was big. We sat
around the living room every evening listening to the singers,
comics, actors and actresses on radio shows. Movies were the
biggest entertainment of all. Sometimes, along with the movie, there
was a stage show, maybe a big band. Most of the time there were two
movies—an "A" movie and a "B"—a double feature. There were
hundreds of them every year. The bills were changed twice a week.

There were a lot of talent contests, feeding the dreams of kids who
thought they could be stars on radio or on film. The "Gateway to
Hollywood" show was a big contest. It was run by Jesse L. Lasky, who
was one of the biggest names in Hollywood. In 1913 he and his
brother-in-law, Samuel Goldfish, and a friend, Cecil B. DeMille,
formed the Jesse L. Lasky Feature Play Company which made a big
hit with its first movie, *The Squaw Man.* (Goldfish later became
Goldwyn.) Many mergers later, the company became Paramount
Pictures, a major Hollywood studio.

Lasky was working for RKO when it was put together with the
"Gateway to Hollywood" contest. The idea of the contest was to find
new young talent around the country, to reward regional winners
with trips to Hollywood, to put potential stars on weekly radio
dramas, and to grant the eventual winners new screen names and
seven-year screen contracts. The names the winning boy and girl
would receive were announced in advance and publicized through-

out the contest so that they would be well known to a listening public, which by then, presumably, couldn't wait to see their favorites on the screen.

The show ran for a year—thirty-nine weeks, actually. It was on every Sunday afternoon and finished at year end. The contest I entered was the third and last of the series. New Year's Eve fell on Sunday that year, 1939, and was the theme of the very last show. The winners would start off the new year with new names and new lives. Fame and fortune were at our fingertips.

There were some complaints during the first two segments about how the contest was conducted. The Wrigley Company was the sponsor, and president Philip Wrigley was so unhappy that Lasky took charge of the show himself the third year, instead of just lending his name to it. Lasky was almost sixty by then, but he traveled across the country conducting the show.

It was never very clear who picked the winners along the way or *how* they were picked. Part of the time they were chosen by talent scouts from RKO and sometimes by audience response. When the group got to Houston, they ran ads in the newspapers inviting interested persons to audition on a certain date. When I went to the tryouts I thought every good-looking boy and girl in the state was there. At seventeen I was one of the youngest, and I was scared half to death.

They gave us parts to read for them. One by one they eliminated different ones of us. I must have read my part fairly well, but I was sure they were on the verge of eliminating me. I could see it on their faces as they listened to me. Several times they hesitated over me before letting me go on. In those few moments I came very close to never having any kind of career at all. Had I been eliminated then, I would not have gone on, ever.

Thrilled and surprised, I was one of the winners. Audience applause determined who went to Hollywood. I got the applause, I remember, but when I was told I was going to Hollywood and going on the radio, I couldn't believe it.

The fact that I was only seventeen and not even through my senior year in high school didn't seem to matter to anyone. This was the opportunity of a lifetime, truly a gateway to Hollywood. My mother would go with me of course. Smother-love. Besides, she was

18

as proud of me as she could be. And anyway, because of my age, the studio had to pay expenses for a chaperone. They sent us train tickets and put us up at the Studio Club, a women-only residence with strict regulations. We were given room and board and $25 a week each in expense money.

The half-hour radio show was divided into three ten-minute segments. Three boy-girl pairs appeared on each show. RKO executives picked anyone, boy or girl, on photographic potential.

The names of the eventual winners were to be Terry Belmont and Gale Storm. And I won. Wow!

One of those who didn't win, Linda Johnson, stayed in town and went on in the business anyway. She's still doing commercials. She married a man named Joe Leighton, and they became Lee's and my two closest friends.

The winning boys were Lee Bonnell, Ned Lefevre, and Bob Brubaker. I know what happened to Lee. He and Ned became very good friends. Ned stayed in the business, but went back to Chicago and into radio. He married Barbara Luddy and worked with her on the old "First Nighter" radio show.

When I walked into the rehearsal hall, the first person I noticed was Lee, standing by the piano. It really was love at first sight. It popped into my head that here was the boy I was going to marry. When I returned to my mother, I told her I'd just met the boy I was going to marry. She said, "Yes, dear, that's very nice." Patronizing. Well, how could she think I was serious? But I was.

I was seventeen. In the little time it took me to get to Hollywood I'd decided I was going to have an acting career and I was not going to marry for five hundred years, or until I was at least twenty-five, whichever came last. But that all changed the moment I saw Lee. He was tall, dark and handsome. He was an older man, but that didn't matter. I figured he was at least twenty. Actually, he was almost twenty-one.

They took me around to introduce me. I said, "How do you do." He said the same thing. He had been in Hollywood a couple of weeks already. He hadn't won the show yet, but there seemed little doubt about it.

After we got to know each other, he told me one day that I reminded him of his little sister. I could have killed him. When someone asked me for a date, I accepted if I could arrange to double with Lee and *his* date. My date and I would be in the back seat of the car. I could see Lee looking in the rearview mirror, upset, as if someone were trying to make a pass at his little sister.

Then one time we triple-dated. The car was crowded, and I maneuvered it so I got to sit in Lee's lap. When he wasn't expecting it, I kissed him. It wasn't the kiss of a little sister. I gave him a kiss he couldn't forget. Soon, we were dating, alone. My mother was concerned, but I didn't care. All I cared about was loving Lee. The working producer of the show, Bobby Brown, and his wife took a liking to us and took us around town. We loved it.

Now I had to worry about both of us winning. We were paired for the final show.

I have listened to a recording of that show many times. The show was corny as it could be. I had a Texas accent you could cut with a knife. When I was pronounced the winner, I was so nervous I couldn't speak, and Lee talked for both of us. I started to cry. I just couldn't believe it.

Now, neither of us would have to go home. We could stay in Hollywood and become stars. Suddenly, Lee Bonnell had become Terry Belmont and Josephine Cottle was Gale Storm. Whoever dreamed up my "Gale" was relating it to "Storm," spelling it as a weatherman would, though I didn't get the connection at first. Well, Gale Storm was better than Josephine Cottle, though I never really changed it, not legally.

I've been Gale Storm for a long time, but my real name, the name I use for business papers, remains Josephine Cottle. Actually, of course, I'm Gale Bonnell, or, to be more accurate, Josephine Bonnell.

Gateway to Hollywood

CBS-Radio network
(Excerpts from the final show, Sunday, Dec. 31, 1939, including the segment featuring Josephine Cottle and Lee Bonnell)

[Music—Up and out.]

ANNOUNCER—*This is the Gateway to Hollywood, the program with a purpose, brought to you by healthful, refreshing, delicious Doublemint gum. The Gateway to Hollywood publicizing the newly created motion picture names Gale Storm and Terry Belmont.* [Applause] *In just a few moments, you will hear six talented boys and girls in their final screen test. Your friendly local merchant is happy to have played a part in making possible this opportunity, just as he is happy to display for your convenience delicious Doublemint gum. Millions daily enjoy this refreshing treat. That's why we say get a couple of packages of healthful Doublemint gum today. You'll like it. And now, Jesse L. Lasky.*

LASKY: *Thank you, ladies and gentlemen. This is the culmination of three months of work for everyone connected with this show. I don't have to tell you how we gathered up boys and girls from every walk of life all over the country. Now, only six are left. Today, from these six, the most talented two will be chosen for whom the names Gale Storm and Terry Belmont have been selected. Yes, before we leave this stage, one boy and one girl will receive new names. They will receive RKO motion picture contracts and actually will become a part of the motion picture industry. They will leap from whatever their jobs were to featured actors in the space of a moment. Their dreams will come true.*

Our judges have been chosen for their experience in recognizing potential screen stars by their acting abilities, personalities, and photographic qualities. I know you're anxious to meet our three lovely young ladies and three handsome young men. So, ladies and gentlemen, from Houston, Texas, Josephine Cottle; from South Bend, Indiana, Lee Bonnell; from Birmingham, Alabama, Aletha Wilson; from Los Angeles, California, Robert Brubaker; from Pittsburgh, Pennsylvania, Sally Cairns, and from Indianapolis, Indiana, Ned Lefevre. Here they are, my friends. They've come from the East, the South, the Southwest, the Middle West, the Far West, seeking possible fame and fortune. And so, my friends, it's time for our radio play to begin. To you boys and girls, let me say simply this: this is your supreme test; work hard every moment you're at the mike, try with all your hearts, for these moments may decide all your futures. I want to hear you at your best today, and may the best boy and girl win. God bless you all.

GALE STORM

ANNOUNCER: *Screen test number 13, brought to you by healthful, refreshing, delicious Doublemint gum. The most talented two will be chosen today to become Gale Storm and Terry Belmont in the radio play "From the Mountaintop," starring the noted screen actor H. B. Warner. Mr. Warner narrates our story.*

WARNER: *High on the mountaintop, man lives. Compared to the universe, he occupies a speck of infinity. Compared to infinity, he lives but a day. But in his day he huffs and he puffs, he rants and he raves, he builds himself up and tears down his world. He sees the sun and the stars, even the heavens themselves, as of no importance compared to himself.*

He does not recognize that moment that will decide the direction of his life. He comes to New Year's Eve with the one he loves best. They talk and they plan the new year and the years to follow, searching for something they do not realize is within themselves. They look for it and they must find it. They do not have much time. Here we take three different couples, facing the future, each looking for something in the new year they have not found in the old.

Here, opening the show, that portion acted by Lee Bonnell and Josephine Cottle:

LEE: *Well, 1939 is almost over.*

JO: *Look down there.*

LEE: *The whole town.*

JO: *The whole world.*

LEE: *Yes.*

JO: *Lee . . .*

LEE: *What, honey?*

JO: *Put your arms around me.*

LEE: *All right.*

JO: *I'm kind of cold.*

LEE: *I know.*

JO: *Do you feel it, too?*

LEE: *A little. It's so big out there, we might get lost.*

JO: *We might.*

LEE: *We won't. But I hope we do. Those who get lost are the ones who are happy. Their light is so little, no one notices them.*

JO: *Ummmm, that's nice.*

LEE: *Before I found you I wanted a big home. I wanted to be rich.*

Now I don't. You know, a man whose life is rich in little things doesn't have to keep on forever stretching out for something more. Men who are lonely are discontented. You're enough to fill my life completely.

JO: *Do you really think I am?*

LEE: *I know it, better than I've ever known anything in my life. Well, the truth is, we're always together, aren't we?*

JO: *Forever, forever, forever. Lee, is there anything . . . oh, I don't know how to explain this . . . but a few minutes ago you seemed so far above me, so much smarter than I am. You understood a lot of things I didn't. You acted like you knew more. You were talking to me the way you'd talk to a little girl.*

LEE: *Did I?*

JO: *Why was that, Lee?*

LEE: *I don't know, Jo. Once when I was young my sister complained about the same thing. I asked Dad why that was. Dad just laughed and said Never mind; it's just the ego of man.*

[Music, indicating time passing.]

LEE: *Well, how do you like being an old married woman?*

JO: *It's too soon to tell yet.*

LEE: *Well, I can answer now. I like it.*

JO: *You do?*

LEE: *Sure. Oh, everything isn't perfect. You should have my slippers ready for me when I come home. And my pipe filled. But I'll train you into that as time goes on.*

JO: *Well, as far as I'm concerned, being married isn't so bad. Of course I was fooled a little. I had an idea you were sweet and thoughtful, but I haven't received a single box of candy since we were married.*

LEE: *You haven't had a box of candy?*

JO: *Not for two whole weeks.*

[Telephone rings.]

LEE: *I'll get it, dear; sit still. Hello . . . who? Annette! How are you? Well, of course I didn't call you. I'm hard to get. . . . How have you been? Are you still a blonde?*

JO: *Who is it?*

LEE: *. . . Well, no, I guess nobody's seen much of me lately. Tonight? Oh, gee, I can't tonight. I've been so busy lately. I've been very busy. Yeah, sure, call anytime, Annette. So long.*

JO: *Lee!*

LEE: *Uhh, what did you say, Jo?*

JO: *Who was that on the phone?*

LEE: *Oh, just a girl I used to go with.*

JO: *Oh, just a girl you used to go with . . .*

LEE: *Yeah. I went with her for about . . .*

JO: *Well, why didn't you tell her you were married?*

LEE: *Why?*

JO: *Lee Bonnell, I'm leaving you!*

LEE: *Jo, you can't do that. I was just kidding her along.*

JO: *Oh, you weren't either. You're tired of me. You're throwing it in my face, right here in our own home.*

LEE: *Why, Jo, I'm doing no such thing.*

JO: *Well, why didn't you tell her you were married?*

LEE: *Why didn't I? Gosh, Jo, I don't know . . .*

JO: *Well, I do! You're just . . .*

LEE: *It just seems like when a girl calls up a fellow for a date she usually likes him pretty well; and, naturally, he hates to hurt her feelings by saying he's all tied up . . .*

JO: *Oh, that's . . . I know, that's some of that ego of man you told me about once, isn't it?*

LEE: *Mad at me?*

JO: *Yes.*

LEE: *Really?*

JO: *I'm so mad at you I could tear you to pieces.*

LEE: *Think you'll ever get over it?*

JO: *I don't know whether I will or not.*

LEE: *Don't you?*

JO: *NO.*

LEE: *Come here.*

JO: *Oh, you crazy . . . oh . . .*

[Music, indicating more passing of time.]

JO: *I have to hang up now, Mother. Lee will be home any minute. We're happier than ever.*

[Hangs up. Thinks:] *Mr. Bonnell, you may take my arm and we'll walk in for dinner. You look very nice tonight, Mr. Bonnell. How do you like me? Well, after all, this isn't something I got out of a barrel. Now, if you'll just sit right there. No, no, there. Oh, we've been married six months and I still love you. Oh, honey, I do love you so much. Oh, gosh . . .*

[Telephone rings.]

JO: *Oh, Lee, it's going to be the swellest dinner any two people ever ate. Could you bring who? You ran into Annette this noon and invited her to dinner? Oh. Oh. Well, all right, bring her home. I told you the table was set for two. I hope you'll enjoy yourselves.* [Click!]

[Music.]

LEE: *Hello.*

JO: *Where's your girl friend?*

LEE: *Oh, I forgot all about her. You're packing your clothes? Are you going someplace?*

JO: *I'm going home to Mother. That's where I'm going.*

LEE: *Well, I can't say I blame you.*

JO: *Well, at least Mother knows how to treat a girl.*

LEE: *Yeh, you're right.*

JO: *All I get here is trouble.*

LEE: *Yes. How did you find out about this evening? It didn't happen until just before I left the office.*

JO: *What didn't?*

LEE: *The boss fired me.*

JO: *Oh, Lee, he didn't . . .*

LEE: *Yep.*

JO: *Oh, honey.*

LEE: *I haven't got what it takes, I guess. I probably never will have.*

JO: *Who says you haven't? The boss doesn't know what it's all about.*

LEE: *Oh, never mind. I'll be all right. You go ahead with your packing.*

JO: *Packing? Do you think I'd leave you when you're in trouble?*

LEE: *But aren't you going home to your mother?*

JO: *Home? Home to my mother when you've just lost your job? Well, I should say not! What you need, Lee Bonnell, is to have that male ego of yours boosted, and I'm just the one who can do it!*

[Music, more passage of time . . .]

LEE: *Well, 1939 is almost over.*

JO: *Lee?*

LEE: *Yes?*

JO: *I'm not afraid anymore.*

LEE: *What do you mean?*

JO: *Well, while we've been standing here I've been thinking I'm not afraid because you seem to know more than I do.*

LEE: *Of course not.*

JO: *It is just your ego. You don't really know so much more; it's just your ego. And it's a woman's place to help you with it, so it never gets too big or too little.*

LEE: *Of course. So let's make a wish on the moon.*

JO: *All right.*

LEE: *You first.*

JO: *Close your ears, Lee Bonnell; this is between the moon and me. Oh, Mr. Moon, you see this boy sitting here beside me? I love him, Mr. Moon. I'm glad he isn't perfect because that makes him human. . . . I've only got one wish: make him love me as much as I love him, and make me love him always as much as I do now.*

LEE: *Finished? Then I'll make mine. Put your hands over your ears, Josephine Cottle. Mr. Moon, there's an awfully pretty girl sitting here next to me. My wish is that she stay just as she is, always. I don't mean sweet all the time. At times I think I love her even more when her eyes flash and she's mad at me. But she's good for me, Mr. Moon. Keep her mine, always, Mr. Moon.*

JO: *Did you make your wish?*

LEE: *Yep. Did you?*

JO: *Yes. What did you wish for?*

LEE: *I won't tell.*

JO: *I'll bet I know.*

LEE: *I bet I know yours, too.*

[Music, up and out. Commercial. The second couple does their scene. Another commercial. The third couple does their scene.]

ANNOUNCER: *You've just heard Gateway to Hollywood, screen test No. 13. . . . And now, once again, here is Jesse L. Lasky.*

LASKY: *In my hands are long-term contracts from RKO studio. They are made out in the names of Terry Belmont and Gale Storm. These names will be the property of the most talented boy and girl, to be chosen in just a few moments by the judges. For thirteen weeks the names have been publicized on these coast-to-coast broadcasts. Hardly a person hasn't heard them. Only when an actor's name is* known to the public is he valuable to a producer or to himself. Therefore, these names are worth many thousands of dollars.

May I say once more, this great opportunity for talented Americans has been made possible by Doublemint gum. Before we find out whom the judges have chosen, I want to present Mr. Grahame Baker. Mr. Baker is co-producer of RKO's forthcoming Tom Brown's School Days. One of the girls from today's program will play a featured role in this new production. Now Mr. Baker will tell us whom he has chosen.

BAKER: *Miss Josephine Cottle.*

LASKY: *Thank you very much, Mr. Baker, and congratulations to Josephine Cottle of Houston, Texas.*

Now, let's move on to the big event of the moment. Gary Breckner, will you take over.

ANNOUNCER: *Very glad to, Mr. Lasky. I want to remind our listeners that the judges are being instructed to cast their ballots from the standpoint of photographic quality, personality, and dramatic ability. And from the deep frowns on their brows and the meditative glances at the ceiling, it would seem that the gentlemen are experiencing a little difficulty in reaching their decision. However, the time is at hand, and I'm going to ask each one of these distinguished judges for his choice for a Gale Storm and a Terry Belmont. The first judge to give his selection is Mr. Perry Lieber, the RKO publicity director.*

LIEBER: *Mr. Lee Bonnell and Miss Josephine Cottle.*

ANNOUNCER: *The second judge is RKO director Frank Woodruff.*

WOODRUFF: *Mr. Lee Bonnell and Miss Josephine Cottle.*

ANNOUNCER: *The third of the judges is RKO producer Eric Palmer.*

PALMER: *Lee Bonnell and Josephine Cottle.*

ANNOUNCER: *And the fourth one is Mel Burns, the RKO makeup expert.*

BURNS: *My choice, like the others, Mr. Bonnell and Miss Cottle.*

ANNOUNCER: *And the fifth judge, RKO talent executive Julius Evans.*

EVANS: *Lee Bonnell and Miss Sally Cairns.*

ANNOUNCER: *And those are the individual votes. And now, Mr. Lasky with the final decision.*

LASKY: *Ladies and gentlemen, here is the final decision. Our new*

Gale Storm is Josephine Cottle. Our new Terry Belmont is Lee Bonnell.

[Applause]

You are indeed to be congratulated. You've made your dreams come true. And now I want you to think of this: Acting is an honorable profession. And it must be kept as such. You owe it to me and to these five distinguished judges, to the RKO studios who will produce your pictures, to the motion picture industry, to Doublemint gum who provided this opportunity, but most of all you owe it to the American public that never, never by any act of your personal or private lives or your public lives will you do anything to mar or hurt these names of Gale Storm and Terry Belmont which I am about to give you. Do you so promise, Josephine Cottle?

JO: *I do.*

[She laughs; the audience laughs.]

LASKY: *I was sure you would. And you, Lee Bonnell, what do you say?*

LEE: *You bet your life.*

LASKY: *Very well, Josephine Cottle, I invest you now and forever with the name Gale Storm. And you, Lee Bonnell, with the name Terry Belmont. Here are your contracts with the RKO studios and your membership cards to the Screen Actors Guild.*

[Applause]

GALE: *Thank you, Mr. Lasky. And hello . . . Terry.*

[Laughs, and the audience laughs.]

TERRY: *Hello . . . Gale.*

LASKY: *Now, listen very carefully, children. You are both to report at 9 o'clock Tuesday morning to Mr. Julius Evans at RKO studios, ready for your first day before the cameras. Now I'm sure we'd all like to hear a word from each one of you. Please.*

GALE [tearfully]: *Well, this is just too much all at once. I just can't express myself . . .*

TERRY [manfully]: *I think we both appreciate it very, very much and want to thank Mr. Wrigley and Mr. Lasky and everybody . . . and . . . . happy new year! It's going to be a swell new year.*

LASKY: *Thank you both. That was very, very nice. Those were lovely speeches. Now, to you, Gale Storm and Terry Belmont, I say, God bless you and good luck to you. What a wonderful start to the new*

*year! To the rest of you talented young folk . . . I have only this to say:
You ran a fine race; your performances were splendid. Having gone
this far—and it is far, indeed—there's no doubt that if you keep
trying, you will have notable careers within your grasp. Keep trying,
and remember, anytime that I can help you or advise you, it would be
my pleasure to do so.*

[Applause]

*Now it's time to say goodbye to all of you. I'm very happy that
today we have completed our talent search and have discovered
another talented boy and another girl who may now move on to
possible fame and fortune in Hollywood. Once again, good luck to our
new Gale Storm and Terry Belmont! And a happy, happy new year to
all of you. This is Jesse L. Lasky bidding you farewell from the
Gateway to Hollywood.*

[Applause]

ANNOUNCER: *And now, here is a personal message addressed only to
the merchants who display and sell Doublemint gum. . . . We ask
you to stay tuned for a private peek at what your new radio show will
be in the coming weeks. The general public is asked to tune out. . . .*

Reprinted by permission of the Wm. Wrigley Jr. Company.

Lee

The contest was great. It brought us to Hollywood, it brought us
together, and it gave us a chance. It was a great big deal in those days,
and it really was a thrill to win, especially since we *both* won.

I was born in 1918. My full name is Everett Lee Bonnell. I'm
from South Bend, Indiana, but I went to Indiana University, not
Notre Dame. My father was a barber. My mother kept house. We
didn't have a lot of money, but we had a lot of love in our family. My
father's name was Lowel Wade and my mother's, Eva Genesie. I
have an older sister, Thelma, and a younger sister, Pati. Pati married
Clare Mayes, who was an All-American football player at Oklahoma
and became a coach in Amarillo. They have two daughters, Susan
and Stacy. Thelma married Donavan Hinkle, a minister, and three

of their four sons—Don, Jr., Danny and Doug—became ministers. David is a history teacher.

I went to South Bend Central High School at the time John Wooden was coaching basketball there in the middle '30s. I was a good-looking young fellow and I knew it. I was very outgoing, very social. I played leads in the school plays. When I went to I.U., I started out with economics, switched to business, then went into the school of arts and sciences because I wanted to concentrate on drama. I got the lead in the first university theater drama I tried out for, which was something for a freshman.

The first play I did was *Silas the Chore Boy*, a real old-fashioned melodrama. Then I was one of the gangsters in *Winterset*, the Maxwell Anderson play. Joseph Hayes played Mio, the lead. He went on to write *Desperate Hours* and some other fine things.

I was still in my freshman year when I heard Jesse L. Lasky's "Gateway to Hollywood" radio show one afternoon. They announced that talent scouts would be in Cincinnati to hold auditions. After two university plays, I figured I was ready. Cincinnati wasn't too far, and I got a friend with a car to drive me there.

When we got to the hotel, there were more than a hundred young fellows trying out for the name of John Archer and more than a hundred young girls trying out for the name of Alice Eaton. I was given a small role to read and waited most of the day to read it for Jesse L. Lasky. When I was called in to read, it was for Bryant Washburn—Lasky wasn't even there. Bryant Washburn was an old silent-screen star who was still playing character roles in movies. He liked what I did and told me to stick around. All day long he was sending boys home, but at the end of the day he told me I'd won. He said I was going straight to Hollywood without even having been on one of their shows. He took my address and said they'd send for me.

The next morning there was a picture of me in the *Cincinnati Enquirer*, and it said I was not only going to be the new John Archer; I was going to be the future Tyrone Power. We went back to I.U., and the university newspaper had picked up the story and I was pictured as the next Tyrone Power. The South Bend paper picked up the picture, and all my family and friends were thrilled for me. I was going to be a star.

I waited for them to send for me. I waited and waited and waited. I listened to the show every Sunday afternoon, and all of a sudden it was the final show in that series and they announced that someone else was the winner of the name John Archer. They had never even sent me a letter. I couldn't believe it. I was badly embarrassed. People kept asking me what had happened, and I just told them I didn't know.

Then one Sunday afternoon, as my cousin and I were playing bridge, "Gateway to Hollywood" came on the air and announced that talent scouts were going to be in Indianapolis; they were going to audition for a new series of dramas—the winners were to get the names Terry Belmont and Gale Storm. They said Jesse L. Lasky himself would be there for the tryouts. Taking my clippings, I hitchhiked to Indianapolis.

This time I was one of the three boys selected to perform before an audience that night at a theater. I won on the basis of audience applause. Mr. Lasky then announced that I would be going to Hollywood to appear on a radio show. Within two weeks I was sent a train ticket. I was, in fact, the first finalist to arrive in Hollywood.

They put me up in the old Hollywood Athletic Club, with my room and board paid for, and gave me $25 a week expense money, which was more than enough in those days. Before Gale got there I was having a great time. I don't mean that the way it sounds, but I was free as the wind. With my first week's "salary" of $25, I bought an Essex coupe with a rumble seat and I went out to the beach every day. I was dating the girls who came out to be on the show. Even the losers stuck around, hoping to catch on with some studio. I was allowed to use the facilities at the club, and I was getting manicures and facials until they cracked down. I was having the time of my life.

When Gale showed up, she reminded me of my little sister. She won her first show and that put her in the semifinals. I was already in the semifinals. Bobby Brown, who was producing the actual shows, put us together for the semifinals; when we won, we were told we'd work together in the final.

I thought Gale was a real cute little gal, but I had become too much of a ladies' man all of a sudden to think of sticking with anyone. I did go on a double date with her, however, and when the guy she was with started to make passes at her in the back seat I couldn't keep

31

my eyes on the road. It really bothered me. After we dropped the girls off, I told the other fellow I thought it was terrible the way he had tried to take advantage of that sweet little girl. He said she might be a sweet little girl, but she was grown up and sexy as all get-out.

The next time we went out she wound up in my lap, giving me kisses I couldn't believe. It hit me like a ton of bricks that I was in love with her, but I really couldn't believe it. Here I was ready to take on all the glamorous movie stars in Hollywood and I'd fallen in love with a pixie from Texas. The chemistry must really have been right. We just seemed right together. I know the other girls told her I was a playboy, and I knew her mother didn't want her to commit herself. But she told me she'd told her mother the first day she saw me she was going to marry me. Once I realized I was in love, there was no doubt about that.

For some reason the show had run short of men for the series, and they asked me if I minded if they brought out Ned Lefevre. I had beaten him in Indianapolis, but they had been impressed by him, too. He already was a big man in Indianapolis—"Old Uncle Ned" Lefevre, with his own radio disc jockey show and all. I was scared to death of his ability, but I liked him, and I couldn't say no when they wanted to give him another chance. We were going to get $125 a week with the contract, and that was plenty of money at that time to take care of two. Ned and I became good friends.

It was more important to me to have Gale win than to win myself, because I was going to stay out here no matter what. Ned and I had agreed that whichever of us won, he would "keep" the other one in Hollywood for six months. Well, when Gale and I won it was wonderful. We were both going to be big movie stars. Ned lost, but I lived up to my bargain. He and I moved into a little hotel near the athletic club, and I supported him for six months while he tried to get a contract somewhere. It must have meant a lot to him. One day after I had left while he was still asleep, I returned to our room and found him unconscious, with the windows closed and the gas heater going. I turned off the heat and threw the windows open and shook him awake. Later, he laughed and said I had not only eliminated him in the contest; I had almost eliminated him for good. Maybe I did leave with the heater going and the windows closed. I don't know that I did, but I took the blame. We laughed it off, but I'll never forget it.

My career didn't come to what I thought it would. Gale had a small part in *Tom Brown's School Days* and the lead in *One Crowded Night* at RKO—and then they dropped her. They called her in and told her she was a nice little ingenue and all that but she just couldn't make it in Hollywood and she'd be wise to marry the guy she was going with, or go home and settle down with somebody else. I think I was more disappointed than she was. She acted as if she'd be content not to be an actress, just to stay out here and marry me and have our children.

At first I worried because they only offered me extra bits, though my contract called for speaking parts. So they put me in a picture called *Too Many Girls*. It had been a George Abbott Broadway hit, and Abbott produced and directed it in Hollywood with Van Johnson and Desi Arnaz and Lucille Ball. It was during the making of this movie that Desi and Lucy got married. I remember they stopped shooting one day to announce that they had run off and married. Someone broke out champagne and we toasted them. Lucy had a ten-cent wedding ring. Desi was a bigger star than she was at the time. They were both nice people. They invited us out to their new house a couple of times.

The studio gave me a bigger part in *Men Against the Sky*, a war movie about airplane pilots. Richard Dix was the star; I had only two or three lines as a pilot who was shot down, but I made an impression, and my option was picked up.

The next year, 1941, I did four films, and it looked as if I might be successful after all. I did *Footlight Fever* with Elyse Knox. We were really attracted to each other, and Gale got jealous—and with good reason. But she was my girl.

Then I did *Parachute Battalion* with Robert Mitchum and Bill Williams and a whole bunch of young male leads they had on the lot at the time. They shot a lot of background material at Fort Benning, Georgia, and we did process shots in the studio, jumping out of planes and hanging from parachutes. The wind machine blew and it looked realistic as could be. World War II had begun, though we weren't in it yet.

After that, I played a gangster in *Lady Scarface*, which starred the great actress Judith Anderson. It was a take-off on *Scarface*, the Paul Muni–George Raft picture about Al Capone.

"B" movies had their niche at the time, and I thought I was going places. To give me added acting experience, the studio sent me to Denver to do a stage play, *The Male Animal*, the big James Thurber Broadway hit. The two weeks I played in it were the longest I had been away from Gale since I'd met her. Her career still hadn't really started. She did only a few westerns that year. It still looked as if I would be the star and she would just be my wife. And when I was called back from Denver because I had been drafted to go into the army, we started to talk about getting married before I'd have to go.

But I didn't have to go—I had terrible eyesight. So I returned to Gale and to Hollywood. The studio thought I would be around awhile, and they gave me the lead opposite Lucille Ball in *Look Who's Laughing*. Edgar Bergen and Charlie McCarthy were in the picture, and Edgar landed Lucy. Lucy was super, and I got to wear a pair of rented tails and top hat in the picture and I really thought I *had* turned into Tyrone Power!

On the 28th of September, 1941, Gale and I were married. She had been living in a two-bedroom apartment with her mother and then with friends and hadn't had a lot of freedom. We went back to Houston for the wedding and a friend of Gale's family who was putting in a tract of houses gave us a $250 down payment on a new little house as a wedding present. We moved Gale's mom into it and told her it was hers for as long as she wanted. We kept up the mortgage on it and supported her. She was very happy to be back among friends and family. She lived there until many years later when she could no longer take care of herself, and we had to put her in a nursing home. I really loved Gale's mother—pioneer stock and a great gal.

Gale was, and is, a great gal, too. For our honeymoon, I took her home to Indiana and showed her off to everyone. My parents were thrilled with her. I had a little convertible and drove around town showing off, no longer Lee Bonnell, just the barber's son, but now a movie star.

On December 7th, Gale and I were back in Hollywood having lunch at the athletic club after church when the waiter came and told us the Japanese had attacked Pearl Harbor. I was pretty patriotic; most people were in those days. My immediate reaction was that now I would definitely have to go into the service, nearsighted or not, to defend my country. Most young men felt that way then.

Joe Leighton, who had married Linda Johnson, one of the contestants on "Gateway to Hollywood," had left public relations at CBS to enter the Coast Guard. He was a chief petty officer, and he offered to help me get in. I thought it was a pretty good idea, but I wasn't taken right away.

I made two more movies in 1942. One was called *Army Surgeon*. The other, called *The Navy Comes Through*, had quite a cast: Desi Arnaz; Pat O'Brien; Jackie Cooper; George Murphy; and Jack Briggs, who later married Ginger Rogers. And Max Baer, the ex-heavy-weight boxing champ whose son became a television star on "The Beverly Hillbillies." The cast used to give poor old punch-drunk Max hotfoots all the time. Pat O'Brien was a good drinker, and he brought cases of Cutty Sark to the set. We used to sit in his dressing room and drink between takes. I never got hooked, but I did develop a taste for good Scotch. Jack Briggs and I became close friends on that film.

Gale got pregnant soon after we were married, and our first child, Phillip, was born the 19th of March, 1942. I was then in the Coast Guard, so she was left at home with the baby. But they didn't take me too far. At first I was sent to Wilmington, which is near Long Beach. I wasn't even given a full uniform. I had a sailor cap, I wore a t-shirt and slacks, I carried a wooden gun, and I guarded the shipyards. It was one of the thrills of my life when I finally got a full sailor suit.

Gale had signed with Monogram by then and was beginning to be known. As men came through Wilmington, I was one of those who assigned them to schools or ships, so I had a little power. I could go home nights and weekends. It was such soft duty that I felt guilty about it, but I would never have been able to shoot anyone I could see, so I wouldn't have been much good in action anyway.

I did put in some time in San Diego and San Francisco and at sea, which took me away from Gale and Phil. Her career really started to take off with a movie in 1944 called *Where Are Your Children?*, a quickie that grossed over a million dollars. It was a big hit and made Gale a star at Monogram. I was happy for her, but also a little jealous. There were stories and pictures of her in all the movie magazines. Sometimes, if I was home, they'd let me get in the pictures, too: "Here is Gale with her actor-husband Lee Bonnell, who is in the Coast Guard."

Most of the men in the service had it a lot worse than I did. The only dying I ever did was in films. But we all wanted to get back to civilian life. Until you establish yourself, movies are a young man's game. Time was passing me by—I was afraid I'd be forgotten. I was. But not by Gale. The war ended. I was discharged. I went back to RKO. Gale and I decided to continue our family, and our second son, Peter, was born the 29th of May, 1946. But by the time I got back to the studio I was not exactly a hot property. New young men had come on by then, and old stars were returning from service, and there just wasn't room for me.

When my option came up for renewal in 1947, I was dropped. My career seemed to have come to a close with eleven films.

A few years later I did a couple of religious movies for Cathedral Films, which played the church circuit. It was a limited audience. For a while it looked as though a major market might develop for these films. I thought I might even make a good living in them. But someone else had other thoughts. I tested for the part of Jesus Christ in one of them. I had the long hair, the beard, the robes, everything; I was perfect for the part. I did the scene in which Christ drives the money-changers out of the temple. As I came down the steps in my sandals and started my speech, I tripped and stumbled and said, "Oh, *hell!*"

They decided I wasn't right, after all.

For a time I tried to get into the production end of the movie business with religious subjects. I was inspired by the story of Bill Alexander, a minister from Oklahoma who came to Hollywood to give a talk and had them in the aisles cheering. Ronald Reagan, who was president of the Screen Actors Guild at that time and belonged to our church, was to follow. I remember saying, "Ronnie, Bill's a tough act to follow." Ronnie smiled and said, "I'll do my best." It was plenty good enough. He had them cheering, too. I never underestimated him after that.

For a while, religion was all I had. I did a lot of soul searching. I did a lot of reading, especially of a little religious book entitled *The Soul's Sincere Desire* by Glenn Clark, which told you how to find yourself. That book was my bible, because I was really looking. I developed a schedule just to fill my days. I'd get up at a certain time, pray at a certain time, exercise at a certain time, read at a certain time. For a while I painted houses. Then I decided to take some courses at Chapman College with the thought of entering the ministry. I seriously pursued that for a time, but, while I was sincere about my religion and knew I could lead people, I lacked confidence in myself: I was afraid of becoming nothing but "Mr. Storm."

Failing in films had taken a lot out of me. I was envious of Gale because her movie career was going so well. She had moved on to Allied Artists and was doing great. She was making $50,000 a year and I was bringing in nothing. She was supporting me. She even bought us our first house. Our third son, Paul, was born in August of 1947. She was supporting our sons. I was serving as her manager. She did need me for that. She was no good with money, so I was handling it. I gave her good advice.

There never was a time when I didn't love her, but there was also a time when I hated her. I was envious of her career and jealous of her life. I mean, she'd made movies with Don Defore, Rod Cameron and George Montgomery!

I started to think that if Gale really loved me she'd stay home and be a wife and mother. If she just stayed home and stopped bringing home so much money, I'd have to go out and make a living for my family. I felt it was Gale's fault that I didn't have more drive and desire. One night we took a long walk and I asked her if she'd give up her career for me. Without hesitation, she said she would. She'd tell her agent to cancel her contracts. It was one of the most marvelous moments of my life. I saw that while she always supported me and never complained about it, she was ready to help me with anything I might want to try. Yet she never asked me to do anything. She always said she was sure I'd find something that was right for me.

I knew she had worked hard to make a success of her career, and I saw how unfair it would be to take that from her. The next morning I told her I didn't want her to give up her career. I really didn't. I told her I just had to be reassured about what was most important to her, and I was grateful for the answer she'd given me. But her career was important to me, too. Ever since then, I've been thrilled by the things she's done. I think she acts and dances and sings beautifully. And she's especially skilled at comedy. She's the most exciting woman I've ever known.

GALE STORM

She also writes poetry. On our tenth anniversary, I got this from her:

> *I searched through rows and rows of cards*
> *With verses by most gifted bards,*
> *And pictures to delight the eye,*
> *And sentiments that made me sigh!*
>
> *But none could quite express the way*
> *My thoughts go—on our special day.*
> *Nor tell the filled-up way I feel*
> *For lovely dreams that you made real.*

I guess you're only human with a mortal flaw or two,
You say you have a temper that your Grandpa gave to you.
There must be other men with wit and charm—to a degree,
But hon, I don't dare tell you the delight you are to me.
You might think "for one girl to have so much cannot be fair,"
And put it on the basis where some other girls would share.
So I'll not lose my head and tell you all I know is true.
I'll merely say I want to live for all my life with you.

I take pride in her. But I had to take pride in myself, too. I had to find something I could do well. I might not have wanted to be a minister, but I did want to serve people in some way. We had friends, Hollis and Vivian Jenkins, who had sort of adopted Gale and me. Hollis was in life insurance, and he always said I was a natural-born salesman. I drew back from that field because I considered it death insurance, but I was desperate, and he convinced me that selling protection to families who needed it was service of the highest order.

He asked me to come down to meet his boss, John Yates, in downtown L.A. Desperate, I went. He was a great salesman himself. He gave me a lot of material to read. The more I read, the more I realized it was a good and an honorable business.

That was about 1950, and I've never been ashamed to ask anyone I knew if I could be of service to them with their insurance needs. I've never used high-pressure tactics and I've never sold anyone anything I didn't think they needed. I was not ashamed to have Gale recommend me to the people she dealt with. By the fourth year I was selling a million dollars' worth of insurance a year, and joined the "Million Dollar Round Table." That's a little like winning an Academy Award. Eventually I was appointed a general agent by Massachusetts Mutual. I recruited my own associates, who are full-time salesmen. They are in business for themselves; I provide the tools, through my agency, for them to be successful. It has been many, many years since I had to be supported by my wife, and there have been many years when I had to support her. Whatever money we have made or make belongs to both of us and is for our family. In my sixties, I am about to change careers. I'll be working as an insurance consultant in helping Gale bring public enlightenment to the problem of alcoholism.

When I look back on the "Gateway to Hollywood" program I do so warmly. It opened doors for me I could not have dreamed of. Above all, it introduced me to Gale. I've been more than happy about the professional life I've created. We have four fine children—our daughter, Susanna, came along on the 12th of November, 1956. Gale and I have been married forty years. All our children are successfully married, too, and we are blessed by five wonderful grandchildren.

4

I remember that at the end of that last "Gateway to Hollywood" show I had to pledge to Jesse L. Lasky and the world on network radio never to do anything in my private or public life to disgrace the name Gale Storm.

I think the talent search was just a gimmick to give them a show that might attract a good radio audience. Since Wrigley paid for it, it didn't cost RKO a cent, but RKO got a lot of publicity. I don't think they expected to get any great talent out of it, and they were able to promote a couple of ringers they rang in. Lee and I never even had a screen test.

They kept Lee for a while, but they never gave him a good part. They needed a supply of young, good-looking leading men or second leads—soldiers for speaking parts in war pictures, for example. He was good, but he never got a really meaty role.

The seven-year contract they talked about so enthusiastically during the show actually lasted six months. RKO was doing well at the time, but it wasn't quite MGM or 20th Century–Fox or Warner's or Paramount. Cary Grant was on the lot then, making those marvelous comedies, but he never made a pass at me.

They did have to tutor my speech, because I had that Texas accent, and *Tom Brown's School Days* took place in England. I lost most of my accent even though I couldn't gain much of an English one.

I Ain't Down Yet

Ginger Rogers was on the lot at that time, too, along with Fred Astaire, making those great musicals. I got to wear Ginger's shorts in *One Crowded Night*. She never knew.

I graduated from high school at a studio school during those six months. Other screen kids in the school were Freddie Bartholomew and Jimmy Lydon and Roddy McDowall. I turned eighteen in April and made those two movies and was ready to become a big star when I was politely told by a studio head that I had no chance to become a big star at all. After two movies and six months RKO had fulfilled its real commitment to me.

They needed a lot of films to fill the double bills in the smaller theaters in those days. Most of the movies I made in the first three or four years I was in Hollywood never played the big theaters. They not only weren't "A" movies, they weren't as good as the "B" movies that played the second half of the bills, at the big theaters. Most of them were made for less than $50,000, including the cost of the film. Some of them were made for less than $25,000. I got $150 a week during the six months I was at RKO, and at first I made $150 or $200 a week when I made a movie at Republic or Monogram or some other small studio. It was a movie a week, and they were called "six-day wonders." The unions eventually got weekends off from production, but in those days we worked Monday through Saturday and we made a movie every week. Sometimes we did more than one movie a week. Sometimes we did one in three or four days. But usually we did them on a six-day shooting schedule, and when the six days were up the movie was done.

I think they took for granted that because I was from Texas I could ride horses. I had ridden horses only a few times in my childhood. One had thrown me, and that gave me a lifelong fear of them. I didn't tell the producers that, of course. A lot of westerns were made in those days. The first picture I made on my own was a western. I made two or three with Roy Rogers at Republic. That was before Dale Evans got on board. The first was *Saddlemates* in 1941. Another was *Red River Valley* in 1942. I think a third was either *Jesse James at Bay* in 1941 or *The Man from Cheyenne* in 1942. All four of these films are on my list, though I don't remember them well.

I remember concentrating very hard to get my lines right so those takes on horseback didn't have to be reshot any more than necessary.

41

Some of the takes were on mechanical horses in front of background screens. In some of the long shots I had doubles, but usually I had to grit my teeth and at least gallop out of or into camera range. Somehow I got by. Once Roy had to sing a song to me while we rode along the trail, preceded by a camera truck. He had different "Triggers," you know, so one didn't have to do all the work, but I think he used the same one in all the close-ups. This one, the real one, was a little too high-spirited to suit me. As we rode along, he kept trying to bite my horse on the neck. As he nipped at him, my horse wanted to shy away and run away, and I had all I could do to hold him in. Good old Roy, lip-synching away, paid no attention. His song seemed to last forever.

After those first two for RKO in 1940, I did six pictures for different studios or producers in 1941, so I was beginning to build credits. It didn't matter how good you were. It didn't matter how good the pictures were, so why would it matter how good the actors were? I could get work on pictures for studios or producers who couldn't afford to keep a lot of top players under contract the way the big studios did. The small producers tended to use the same people over and over again because they were reliable. I was reliable. I did what I was told to do. I didn't have to be temperamental.

After I did a western at Republic early in 1942, I applied for a musical at Monogram. Lindsley Parsons was the producer. He was a powerful figure at Monogram—a stern man who always sat behind a big cigar, saying little and daring you to sell yourself during an interview. I had hay fever the day I went to see him—my eyes were red and watering, my nose was dripping, and I spent the entire interview with a man's handkerchief to my face, sniffling and sneezing. One bright, beautiful gal after another had gone in to see him, and I figured I didn't have a chance.

So I couldn't have been more surprised when I got the part. The picture was *Rhythm Parade*, and I guess I did all right because Lindsley Parsons then offered me a seven-year contract to do pictures for him at Monogram. It started at $300 a week, and I grabbed it because it represented security. It had been a hassle, going from one audition to another. It hadn't worked out at RKO because my contract there was merely a prize for winning a contest, but I thought a contract at Monogram would work out because I was wanted on the basis of work I had done. There still were those six-month options, but I would be working, not waiting. My agent thought I should take it. So did Lee. So I took it.

And I never regretted it. At RKO I could only have been a small fish in a big pond. Monogram didn't make "A" movies, and the "B" movies it did make didn't play the big chains because the majors made their own "B's." Monogram wasn't even in competition with Columbia, Universal, or RKO, which operated on some middle ground. Monogram was in competition in the minors with Republic for room in the small houses. Their movies never saw downtown in a day when the major movies played their first runs downtown before dropping down to the neighborhood theaters.

Originally, Monogram made mostly westerns—with Tim McCoy, Tex Ritter, and, before I got there, John Wayne. Republic, meanwhile, had Gene Autry, Roy Rogers, Johnny Mack Brown, and, for a while, John Wayne. Later, Johnny Mack Brown came to Monogram to do "straight" roles. Republic's straight stars included John Carroll, a supposedly singing Clark Gable; and Vera Hruba Ralston, wife of company president Herb Yates.

Monogram also did the early Charlie Chan films and the "Bowery Boys" movies. I never did a Charlie Chan, but I did films with his Number One son, Keye Luke. The Bowery Boys were the Dead End Kids from the stage hit.

Monogram made a lot of movies that were better than people remember, a lot better than they might have been, considering what we had to work with. Many were fun to do and fun to watch. I was embarrassed by some of them, but not all by any means, and I was never embarrassed by my work in them—never. I ran the danger of being typed as a "B" actress, but I enjoyed my work and didn't worry about it.

About a year after I was hired and had gotten to know Lindsley Parsons better, I got up the courage to ask him why I had been hired when I was in such bad shape. He told me, "The others I auditioned were so obviously trying to make a big impression on me that I was bored by them. You acted so much as if you didn't care, as if you might even turn down the part if offered it, that I was intrigued by you. You had that cold or hay fever or whatever and didn't try to cover it up. You were natural. I'd seen your work and thought you were a natural. So you were the one I went for."

I did try to make the most of it. When I saw the stills that were made of me when I won the "Gateway to Hollywood" contest I was not happy with them, because my smile was so broad that it showed my upper gums, and that was unattractive. I concentrated on it for a long time, trying to correct it, smiling in front of a mirror until I had reduced the gum line to a reasonable level. After a while I had so perfected my new smile that I couldn't have smiled the old way even if I'd tried. I worked on the things that a diction coach had taught me until I could speak without my Texas accent though I still tended to talk fast.

One day I asked if I could see the rushes of the scenes that had been shot the previous day on a picture. Usually the producer and director and cameraman and people like that checked these over every day to see where they were and how they were doing and to get an idea of which shots from each scene they'd keep when they cut the picture into its final form. Usually, however, the actors were not permitted to look at these rushes because they weren't concerned about the picture; they cared only about their own parts in it. They would see things they didn't like, and they'd complain and want the scenes reshot, which was costly. They didn't take nearly so many shots of each scene of a Monogram "B" picture as they would of a Metro "A" picture. They weren't nearly so demanding; their standards weren't nearly so high. They didn't have the chance to make so much money, so they didn't have the money to spend. They didn't have to cater to the whims of their stars, because their stars were replaceable.

Lindsley Parsons saw that I was sincere. I explained that I just wanted to see what I was doing so I could see where I needed improvement, but that I'd keep it to myself; I wouldn't say a word to anyone. So he said all right, as long as I behaved myself. And I did. It is difficult to watch yourself on screen. You are very aware of yourself and very self-conscious. Some actors can't take it and so never watch themselves on screen. But I needed to watch myself in action. I didn't like a lot of what I saw back in those early days, but I tried to be objective and realistic about it so I could learn from it. I watched the way I moved. I studied my facial expressions. I listened to the way I spoke. What I didn't like, I worked on until it was more nearly what I wanted. I eliminated mannerisms I didn't like, for example. If the people who say "you know" at the end of every sentence would listen to themselves they wouldn't do it.

I listened to my directors. I was respectful of them. Most of them were pros who knew what they were doing. They did the best they could with what they had. I finally got up enough courage to make suggestions. If a line didn't seem right to me or for me, I'd politely ask if I could say this or that instead, and eventually they came to accept most of my suggestions. I never made a big deal of it. I'm not a writer. In fact, if someone criticized a script or a movie, I would usually say, "I don't know, because I'm not a writer." But no actor ever lived who didn't think he knew something about lines.

I listened to my fellow actors. I worked on one film with Jackie Cooper, who had been a star since childhood. One time, while they were setting up for another shot of an emotional scene, I was talking to the crew when Jackie called me aside and pointed out that if I was going to go right back into the same intense scene and hoped to hold the same emotional level, I should go off by myself, stay in character, and concentrate on my part. I could let down that night, but not during the day's shooting. I thought that was good advice and followed it ever after. And I must say my shots matched up much better from then on.

I worked very hard. There wasn't as much waiting around on those pictures as there usually is in movies or as there is now in television. They didn't take the time to carefully set up each shot. Those films ran sixty to seventy-five minutes, and you had to get ten to fifteen minutes of usable footage every day. In the majors they may take ten days of shooting to get ten good minutes, but we were minor league. The directors weren't artists; they were traffic cops. They told you where to go and when to get there. You didn't rehearse a shot—you shot it. You hit the mark or you messed up.

They didn't have a lot of stars. Each one of their stars was in just about every shot of every film. You didn't sit around waiting for one of your shots; you did the shot. The story, the lines, the plots, the setups were as simple as possible. I didn't read my scripts; I learned them. By watching everything and working hard at it, I learned a lot about myself and about the mechanics of making motion pictures. I learned about levels of dialogue and camera angles. I learned such things as how to match shots, which the average person doesn't even think about. Often they shoot ten seconds of a scene, then twenty seconds, and so forth. They shoot it from different directions. You have to be in the same position, holding your hands and your head and so forth in the same way so that one shot in a scene is matched by the next. You have to be speaking in the same way. I got so I could do it every time.

I'd go home exhausted at the end of the long day, grab some dinner, memorize my lines for the next day, tumble into bed, and fall asleep. And I'd get up early the next morning and rush off to the studio to start another long day. I'd work six days, take Sunday off, then be back at it on Monday. I had married Lee in 1941, and I took time off in 1943 to have our first baby, but I didn't take much time off before I was back at work, leaving the baby, Phil, with a sitter. Diverting entertainment was in demand, and we provided it.

I had made six movies in 1941 and I made six more in 1942. One I remember was *Lure of the Islands*, which was shot in the studio. They threw up a few thatched huts and palm trees and we were on an island. One of the stars was Margie Hart, a famous stripper in those days. We wore grass skirts and grass bras. Apparently, the weaving on Margie's bra wasn't tight enough, and under the bright lights the real Margie began to show through. The director stopped shooting and hesitantly explained the problem to Margie and told her they'd have to rework her bra before they could proceed. She said OK, took off her bra and handed it to him! You could have heard a pin drop on that set. They might take that sort of thing in stride today, with nude scenes and all, but they sure didn't in those days. It didn't mean anything to Margie, but it meant a lot to the men on that set. It was all they talked about for weeks.

Without taking off *my* bra, I got good reviews in most of my movies. The movies themselves got better reviews than you might imagine, especially from the trade papers like *Variety* and *The Hollywood Reporter*, which were read by the people who booked films into the theaters and by the theater owners who bought them. There were some terrible turkeys, but Lindsley Parsons's productions were better than many others of their kind. He used good directors who knew what they were doing, and he got good performances out of good performers.

Reviews

Where Are Your Children?

"A strong story of juvenile delinquency, this surprising package from Monogram is one of the sleepers of the year. Jackie Cooper gives his best performance since his early years and Gale Storm gives her best performance yet. The supporting cast is excellent. This one should do big business wherever it plays."

The Hollywood Reporter

Freckles Comes Home

"This has enough action to please everyone, all the ingredients of a hit. Gale Storm proved her talent contest victory of a few years ago was no mistake. She scores heavily here."

Variety

Campus Rhythm

"Gale Storm is stardom bound. This cute and cunning actress, now singing and dancing, steals the show, and it's a pleasant, tuneful show that is a joy to watch."

Hollywood Reporter

Nearly Eighteen

"Disguising herself as a child prodigy of 14 at a talent school, the 21-year-old Gale Storm is pleasantly acceptable. She appears ready to be going places."

Hollywood Reporter

Forever Yours

"The most ambitious movie yet made by Monogram, this movie is of high quality, especially for this studio. It is done in distinctive taste. It is excellent. Its long list of veteran stars is excellent. Keeping company with these stars, Gale Storm outshines them all. She gives a vividly moving performance. The brilliance of this performance stamps her as star material, unquestionably."

Hollywood Reporter

Sunbonnet Sue

"If they gave Academy Awards for independent studio productions, this Monogram musical would be a sure winner of an Oscar. No ordinary low-budget movie, this is one of the pleasantest musicals of the year. The rare and radiant Gale Storm is a wonderful little actress."

Los Angeles Herald-Express

G.I. Honeymoon

"Gale Storm is a delight in this pleasant little comedy. She takes to comedy like a duck takes to water. Her star has been hidden in small movies, but she is really starting to shine through."

Hollywood Reporter

Swing Parade of 1946

"Someone knows his music. Here they have hit a previously unmatched high in Monogram products. Gale Storm has been working on her career, and her efforts show."

Hollywood Reporter

"A tuneful delight and excellent entertainment. Interest rests primarily in Miss Storm, as both singer and actress. Her timing is excellent in her light moments. She delivers strongly on four songs. Her numbers are particularly good."

Variety

It Happened on Fifth Avenue

"With Monogram having reorganized as Allied Artists, this movie is another move toward the big time. This is brilliant entertainment. Victor Moore heads a marvelous cast of veterans. Young Gale Storm is very lovely and effective."

Hollywood Reporter

The Dude Goes West
"This is a wonderful western, offbeat, funny, and remarkably real. Eddie Albert is superb, a clever comic actor. Gale Storm is wonderful."

Variety

The Kid from Texas
"A routine western, with Audie Murphy, the war hero, the hero here. Gale Storm is lovely as his wife. She makes a real characterization of the role, more so than is written in the script."

Hollywood Reporter

Al Jennings of Oklahoma
"Gale Storm is a standout in this western with Dan Duryea. The Technicolor photograph reveals her full beauty, which matches her plentiful physical attributes. Showing great charm and poise, she manages to make her character believable, a major trick."

Hollywood Reporter

The Underworld Story
"This story of crime has excellent production values and outstanding performances by Dan Duryea, Herbert Marshall, Gale Storm and others. Miss Storm is a fine dramatic actress as well as a fine comedic actress and excellent singer and dancer. She is a beautiful lady and a multitalented one. She has not been used as well as she might have been."

Hollywood Reporter

5

Monogram wanted to move up to the big time. If it did, I would go with that. *Where Are Your Children?* was an ambitious step in that direction. It was a story about juvenile delinquency, and not many like that had been done back in 1943. It wasn't the best story in the world, but it was better than the ones I had been doing. They gave it ten days and spent $70,000, which was almost twice the usual. Jackie Cooper was in it, too. It got razzle-dazzle promotion, with big ads in all the newspapers and magazines. It got really good reviews and made more than a million dollars.

Suddenly major studios wanted me. Parsons had sold my contract to Monogram for maybe $10,000, which was pure profit for him. MGM wanted to buy my contract from Monogram, but they wouldn't sell. It did offer to sell half my contract and share my services, but only RKO was interested in such a deal. It would have been ironic if the studio that had dropped me so fast had grabbed me back. But the deal fell through. The hold that even small studios had on their contract players at that time was so strong that the performer was powerless to control his or her own career.

Wanting me to be happy, Monogram did jump my salary to $1,000 a week for 40 weeks of work a year, then to $1,250 a week about a year later, so I was making $50,000 a year by then.

In 1944, I got to star in the most ambitious movie Monogram had made. It was originally called *They Shall Have Faith*, then retitled

Forever Yours. It was produced by Jeff Bernerd and directed by Bill Nigh. It featured the biggest stars Monogram had around—Sir Aubrey Smith, Johnny Mack Brown, Johnny Downs, Conrad Nagel, Frank Craven, Mary Boland—experienced, capable performers. I had the best and most dramatic part I'd ever had, as a polio victim who marries her doctor.

The next year, I did *Sunbonnet Sue*, a musical, and *G.I. Honeymoon*, a comedy, so I was getting to run the gamut of roles in those years. My co-star in *Sunbonnet Sue* was Phil Regan, a real rascal, as I will explain shortly. *G.I. Honeymoon* gave me my first comedy part of the kind I'd get later in television, and I loved it. It was fast and funny, and it did well.

Lee was discharged from the service in 1945 and tried to rekindle his flickering career, but without much luck. We did have our second son, Peter, in 1946.

I made only one movie in 1947, *It Happened on Fifth Avenue*, and one in 1948, *The Dude Goes West*. But those were the two best movies I ever made and by far the two best remembered. They are among the ones that still play on television. If I didn't have a list of all the movies I've made, even I wouldn't remember many of them. Most of them simply filled out double bills and served as a diversion for a war-weary world. But a few weren't bad. And these two were the best. Both were produced by Allied Artists, a Monogram subsidiary, which it had formed to make major movies that wouldn't be embarrassed by the Monogram banner.

I had just had our third son, Paul, and was still in the hospital when I was brought the script of *It Happened on Fifth Avenue*. It was a very warm and funny story about a bum who makes the best of two possible worlds by living in vacant millionaires' mansions in the North during the summer and the South during the winter.

Victor Moore, that marvelous old stage actor and comedian, played the bum, and I played the daughter of a millionaire who discovers Victor and his friends living in my dad's mansion but doesn't tell him who I am or anyone else who he is. Charlie Ruggles, another wonderful old actor, played my father, and the great Mary Boland was my mother. The young male leads were Johnny Mack Brown and Don Defore. Don and his wife became dear friends of ours. He later played the next-door neighbor in the "Ozzie and Harriet" TV series. He was a super performer.

Academy Award winner Frank Capra had bought the story for his Liberty Productions but turned it over to Allied Artists. Unfortunately, he didn't direct it. Roy Del Ruth produced and directed it. I still feel so strongly about it that I must tell you he hurt it terribly. And he hurt *me* terribly. I had two songs to do, and I was very excited. I'd done songs in other movies, but they were low-budget productions. The sky was the limit in this one, and I figured my numbers would have high values.

Almost as soon as I got out of the hospital I started to rehearse the songs and choreography. Then I was notified by an assistant to the director that someone else would sing my songs for me and I'd simply lip-synch them. I couldn't believe it. I thought that maybe the director didn't know I'd been singing and dancing in films, and that if I spoke to him he'd let me do my own numbers. Well, I asked him, and he said no. I asked him to look at some of my musicals, and he said no. I asked him if I could sing for him, and he said no.

His theory was that if you were a dancer, you didn't sing; if you were a singer, you didn't dance; and if you were an actor, you didn't sing *or* dance. It was humiliating.

I wasn't the only one Del Ruth humiliated. Victor Moore was a dear sweet old man who was kind to everyone; we all loved him. Except Del Ruth. Whatever Victor did, the director made him redo it—again and again. And Del Ruth never told the old man what he might have been doing wrong.

The Dude Goes West was a routine story about an eastern dude who tries to make it in the West in the cowboy days, but the characters were strong, the lines were good, and the comedy was intelligent. Eddie Albert played the dude, while I played the love interest. He was wonderful to work with, as good as any co-star I ever had. You bounce your lines off your co-star, you know, and he can make you better. He was one of the best. Also in the cast were James Gleason, Gilbert Roland, and Barton MacLane. Kurt Neuman's direction was skilled and sympathetic. He was a delight to work with.

But *It Happened on Fifth Avenue* and *The Dude Goes West,* while they got very good reviews and pulled in business, did not do for Allied Artists what the studio expected. It was still difficult for the studio to get its product into the first-run theaters or on top of double bills, and these movies didn't make much money. The war was over, television had come into existence, and the movie business was bad. Double bills were on their way out, and the demand for "B" movies was declining drastically. I got good reviews from both movies— really good reviews, in fact—but I had not made the move to a major studio in time. I was stamped as a "B" actress at a time when there was little demand for "B" performers.

I made only one movie for Allied Artists in 1949, and that was the eighteenth and final one I made on the Monogram lot. It was a western, *Stampede*, with one of the better "B" actors, Rod Cameron. Rod was a wonderful fellow, and he and his wife were friends of ours for a while. We noticed that her mother was always with them, and one day Rod left his wife to marry his mother-in-law. Circumstances produce strange situations both in and out of Hollywood.

A few years later, Allied Artists drifted into television production. I let my seven-year contract expire in 1949 and moved on. My movie career continued for a few years before I, too, got into television, but it never really came to what it might have.

6

E ventually, I had to hire a secretary to handle the fan mail and
requests for pictures that came in every day. She kept
scrapbooks, and I have dozens of them, bulging with stories. I
was the cover story many times of every movie magazine published in
those days, and there were dozens. I was the cover story of most of the
women's magazines. I was on the cover of *Look* magazine wearing a
swimming suit. I posed in every kind of costume for every kind of
publication you can imagine. Why, I have a dozen photos of myself
and my young sons dressed up as bunny rabbits, and I can't for the life
of me remember what for. I modeled dresses and shorts and play wear
for fashion layouts. I did ads for clothes, hair preparations, and nail
polishes.

I took promotional tours all across the country, giving interviews
to every newspaper in the land ("Gale Storm in Town with New
Movie," "Lovely Star Takes Our Town by Storm," "Glamorous Gale
Down-to-Earth Gal"). Much was made of my goody-goody image
("Actress Gale Storm Doubles as Sunday School Teacher,"
"Glamorous Movie Star To Spend Most of Her Easter in Church,"
"God Is Number One with Gale," "Family Comes First for Star"). A
flower was named after me by the Hollywood Garden Club—a
blue-bearded iris, of all things.

I didn't know how to deal with all this, but I learned as I went
along. I remember on one occasion when Lindsley Parsons took me

Baby Jo: Here I am,
Josephine Owaissa Cottle,
six months old, 1922.

Ernest A. Bachrach, Radio Pictures

Above: With the famed
Jesse L. Lasky, movie
pioneer and guiding
light of the "Gateway to
Hollywood" contest. I
was seventeen.

Lee and I, the new winners of the "Gateway to
Hollywood" contest, are welcomed to RKO
studios by comedian Joe Penner.

Lee and I, on the pier at Laguna, before our marriage.

Mom and I, six months after my arrival in Hollywood, 1940.

Above: On our wedding
day with my maid of
honor, Virginia
Christenson, and Lee's best
man, his brother Jack.

Here I am, the happy
bride, gathering marriage
congratulations in front of
our first home.

Above: *Being from Texas, I was supposed to be an expert horsewoman. Here I get a boost into the saddle from my friend Betty Anderson Noble.*

With my first costar, Roy Rogers.

Above: Home from the high seas (a base about forty miles from home), Coast Guardsman Lee Bonnell greets his bride.

Stripper Margie Hart and I are the "Lure of the Islands." She is wearing her bra at the moment.

Lee and I admire our third son, Paul, shortly after his birth in the fall of 1946.

I make it look easy to admire this lady's child during an "Oh! Susanna" episode. That's because it really is my own daughter Susanna. Captain Roy Roberts looks on.

Left: *I guess I done bad. Rory Calhoun seems to think so, anyway, and Rod Cameron doesn't disagree. The movie is* Stampede, 1949.

Above: *On the lone prairie with Rod Cameron in* Stampede.

"Sunbonnet Sue," sweet as I can be, 1945.

A *publicity still from my*
1950 film, The Underworld
Story.

Above: *Donald O'Connor is my*
dancing partner in Curtain Call at
Cactus Creek, *1950.*

Left: *I think Howard Da Silva*
suspected me of trying to steal a
scene from him in The
Underworld Story.

to lunch, I started to butter a roll and he stopped me and told me how. I was to put the roll on the small dish, break off a small piece, butter it over the plate, eat it daintily, then, after an appropriate interval, break off another small piece. . . . I was taught how to act so I could live up to the image that was created for me. The goody-goody image I created for myself simply by being honest with interviewers about my personal priorities. The studio could live with that, because those were the kinds of roles I played on the screen. But I did get the big buildup. I was sent on promotional tours, entertained at service camps, visited wounded young men in hospitals. I appeared at premieres and at openings for everything from supermarkets to nightclubs.

I ran across an old story recently which said, "Gale has an understanding with the studio that whenever she is going to have a baby she does no work before the camera." I think I was wise in this, don't you? I didn't let them photograph a single birth of mine. But the minute the baby was born, before we even got out of the hospital, they were shooting pictures of us. In my scrapbooks there are layouts of me with each of my three sons when they were just born, when they were one, when they were three, when they were five; first one child, then two, then three.

The fact is that Lee and the children mattered more to me than my movie career. I loved Lee very much; I was only nineteen when I married him. It was an enormously emotional moment for me. We went back to Houston, to my family. I started crying the morning of the wedding and didn't stop for three days. When I cry, I'm a mess. I cried so much that Lee got truly concerned and asked me, "Honey, did you really want to get married?" Through my sniffles, I assured him I really did. I finally got control of myself and stopped crying. Until we went to South Bend to meet his mother and father. I was so touched by the warmth with which they received me that I started to weep all over again.

I wanted to have a home of my own.

When we were married, we moved into an apartment near downtown Hollywood. It was a nice place, but small: it had only one bedroom. When our first baby was born we moved into a two-bedroom apartment in a sort of U-shaped complex on Orange Street. After the war, when our second baby was born and I was beginning to make pretty good money, we rented a furnished house in Studio City in the San Fernando Valley, and that was our first real house. It had a backyard for the kids and a barbecue and things like that, so we started to live like southern Californians.

When our third child was born we bought a house for the first time, farther into the Valley. It was small, but it was a nice place and we added onto it. We lived there six or seven years. We rented a cottage with a boat on Lake Arrowhead for the summers and spent weekends and whenever else we could on the water. We were leading a pretty good life, if not the glamorous one you associate with Hollywood. We went to some parties and met some important stars, but we weren't party people, and our good friends weren't the great stars.

When we first got married we didn't want children right away. This was before birth control pills, so I went to a doctor and was fitted with a diaphragm. After examining me the doctor said I had an upside down uterus—he called it an "acrobatic uterus," which I loved—and Lee's sperm could not possibly make it upstream to be fertilized. So there was no way I could become pregnant. Nine months later I was. The doctor couldn't believe it. Then he told me regretfully that there was no way I could carry the baby to term. Nine months later Phil was born. The doctor said the birth was a miracle. After Lee returned from service, I had another miracle, Peter; and fourteen months after that, Paul. I guess my acrobatic uterus got tired of turning tricks then, because it was almost ten years before I had our fourth, Susie.

I think that one of the things Lee and I always had going for us was that we were real down-to-earth people before we were swept up by the excitement of Hollywood.

When we were married, we shopped for a church as much as we did for a home. We shopped for a church the way married people with children shop for schools when they're shopping for a new home. Originally, we joined Hollywood Beverly Christian Church. We didn't wear it on our chests like a medal, but we both believed that practicing our religion was the basis of a good marriage. We wanted to pass on this belief to our children. We did. We went to church, and they went with us. They were sent to Sunday School. I do not believe in forcing my beliefs on others. But if young people are not exposed to religion there is no way they are going to develop an understanding of it.

Eventually, some of our kids drifted away. This seems to happen to many youngsters as they get "sophisticated." But they have now returned to the church. This happens often, too. I think as they get older their religion will grow. Ours has. As we have passed through illnesses and chapters of crisis, God has given us the strength to get through it all, and we have come to feel closer to Him than ever before.

I didn't mind that the fan magazines wrote about my religion. It was the truth and I wasn't embarrassed about it. And I don't care if it's unfashionable now.

Lee originally belonged to one of the Churches of Christ. I was brought up in St. John's Methodist Church, and that was where we were married. Eventually, we landed in the Bel Air Presbyterian Church out here, and here we have remained. The Reagans belong. Donn Moomaw, the former All-American football player from UCLA, is the pastor and is an inspirational speaker. But I don't think the particular church matters. We believe, and we practice our belief. We give to the church and do for the church. I taught Sunday School for years. We have tried to teach our children the Christian beliefs that we've tried to practice in our lives. I'm no saint, but I think a few angels have watched over me along the way.

Perhaps Lee and the kids occasionally felt neglected because of my career, especially in the early days. When Lee was in service, I left Phil with a nurse every day. I think as the kids grew up they resented the career that took me away from them, but I believe that in time they understood how much my career meant to me. Lee understood. Maybe we could have been happy with the simple life in a small town, but I'm sure I've been happier having had a screen career as well as a good family life and a happy home. Once I got into it, I found out how happy I was as a performer, how much it meant to me to perform. The applause and the praise were nice, but it was the performing that mattered most.

Sometimes one good part can give you the break you need. I think the part I had in *Where Are Your Children?* kept my career alive and gave it the momentum it needed. If I had gotten a major studio contract out of it, I might have become a major star. But I might have gotten lost on a big lot. I might never have gained the particular credentials that enabled me to land the part in television that did make me a big star. And made us a lot of money and gave us a good life.

For a while I was supporting the family. I saw how much that hurt Lee; it hurt terribly. A man hates to have a woman paying the bills. A man hates to ask a woman for money. I hurt for Lee. I didn't care about the money. I was happy I was making it. What was mine was his, ours. But I was supporting our sons, and that really got to Lee. All I could do was make light of it, encourage him to keep going, and proclaim my faith in him.

I had agents and accountants, but I asked Lee to manage me. I could add and subtract, but I didn't really know much about money. The fact is I've let Lee take care of the arithmetic so long I've now forgotten how to add and subtract. And I have never gone wrong with any career advice he has ever given me. He is wise in that way.

Lee may have envied me my life away from home, then, but he had little to be jealous about. Maybe because I was stamped as goody-goody Gale, I got work without once being shown the casting couch. No producer ever chased me around his desk. After a while, in fact, I started to wonder if something was wrong with me. I wanted to be a temptress. I would have said no, but I wanted to be asked. Finally, after I made a few films with Phil Regan, I discovered I had stumbled onto a real wolf. He had become a sort of family friend, and once he stayed overnight. I remember Lee looking at us funny when I drove off to the studio with Phil the next morning. He drove me home the next night, but stopped on the way at a scenic spot, parked, and really went after me. I resisted mightily, but we got back to the house late and Lee was clearly concerned. He was suspicious, but for a long time I didn't tell him what happened.

Years later, I made a movie with George Montgomery, now Dinah Shore's ex. He had a ranch furnished with a lot of the things he'd made himself, and when we had to take publicity stills for one of the pictures, he talked them into doing them at his ranch. When the publicity people left he showed me his wood work. If I could have gotten my hands on one of his six-guns, I'd have plugged him. Lee was suspicious of George, too.

Look, Phil was a macho Irish tenor. George was a handsome devil. You can't kiss a girl on camera, I suppose, and not think she wants to be kissed off camera as well.

One day when Lee and I went for a walk he asked me if I would give up my career for him. I said I would; I wouldn't have hesitated for a moment. If it was that important to him, fine; it wasn't that important to me. He was finding it a temptation to take it easy while I was working; if I weren't working, he would have to work. If he needed motivation, the least I could do was give it to him. And I don't think I would have regretted it too much. I would never have known what I had missed.

I think he would have sensed it if I hadn't been sincere, but I was. I told him I'd call my agent the following morning to tell him to cancel my contracts because I was retiring. I would have, too. Someone else would have been our little Margie. But he lay awake all night thinking about it, and before I could call the next morning, he told me not to. It was sweet, teary, loving.

Before long he was launched on a career in insurance. Before long he was big in the business. It turned out to be just right for him. He is personable and sincere; he works hard and well. He created his own agency and built a new business life for himself. I am as proud of him and his career as he is of me and mine. I help him in his career and he helps me in mine.

7

One day I let my contract at Allied Artists expire and the next day I signed with Universal. The money was about the same, but it was a better studio. It competed with Columbia on some middle ground. But it was an old studio which had had Rudolph Valentino, Lon Chaney, and Wallace Reid in the silent days and had scored with Boris Karloff and Bela Lugosi in *Frankenstein* and *Dracula* in the early thirties.

In the late thirties and forties it scored with Deanna Durbin in a series of musicals, Abbott and Costello in a series of comedies, and Maria Montez, Turhan Bey and Sabu in a series of exotic adventure films. When I signed in 1949 the studio's stars included Donald O'Connor, Jeff Chandler, and Tony Curtis. It needed female love interest and musical leads, and I figured I'd get good roles in films that were a cut above "B's," if not quite the highest of "A's."

I was so busy I couldn't believe it. The contract gave them the right to loan me out, and I made five films in six months. I had excellent leading men. Dan Duryea, who always seemed so sneaky on the screen, was a very gentle man. I don't think Audie Murphy's heart was in his work, but Edmond O'Brien was an exceptionally strong actor. They put a fair amount of money into the productions, put good directors on them, and took a little time with them—maybe three weeks instead of one. They worked hard on each scene, and it showed on the screen. They weren't great, but they weren't too bad.

The demands on me were much greater. Not just at the studio, but at home, too. The kids were growing up and I wasn't with them enough. Lee was just getting going and I wasn't with him enough. I'd get up at the crack of dawn, grab breakfast, rush to the studio, get home late at night, grab dinner, study lines, and fall asleep exhausted. But the films weren't *that* good. I wasn't really getting anywhere.

Lee started me thinking about retiring, and the more I thought about it the more attractive it looked to me. I wasn't really ready to retire, but I was ready to get off the merry-go-round. I thought it might be better if I weren't a contract player anymore, assigned to whatever a studio wanted me to do, whenever they wanted me to do it. So I asked Universal to let me out of my contract, and they did. I cursed them for not kicking up a fuss.

Columbia was interested in me, and I thought it might be better over there. Run by the dictatorial Harry Cohn, it boomed with the Frank Capra comedies in the '30s and '40s, and had blockbuster hits in *Gilda*, with Rita Hayworth and Glenn Ford; *The Jolson Story*, with Larry Parks; *All the King's Men* with Broderick Crawford; *Born Yesterday* with Judy Holliday; and *From Here to Eternity*, with Burt Lancaster, Montgomery Clift, Frank Sinatra, Deborah Kerr, and Donna Reed. I signed for a couple of pictures with them in 1951, thinking I'd get something great. Instead, I got *Al Jennings of Oklahoma*, with Dan Duryea, and *The Texas Rangers*, with George Montgomery. Back in the saddle again—though I took pride in doing *Curtain Call at Cactus Creek*, with Donald O'Connor, Eve Arden, Vincent Price, and Walter Brennan.

In 1952, I went back to Republic to do *Woman of the North Country* with Rod Cameron. It was just a piece of work. I didn't know it would be the last movie work I would ever do. I would not have remembered it or that it was the last picture I made if I hadn't looked it up. But it was the thirty-fourth and final film on my list, twelve years or so after I started at RKO.

I could have gone on working, but it wouldn't have been worthwhile. Money didn't matter that much to me. My family really mattered more. So I walked off the lot after my last scene, walked into the front door of my house, and prepared to be a housewife. I was thirty years old and I had sons who were ten, eight, and six. I really thought I was ready to retire.

Television came along and unretired me in a hurry.

8

D own deep, I was discouraged by the way my movie career had gone. I was happy with a lot that I had done, but unhappy that I hadn't gotten to do better. I was serious about settling down to home and family, but I felt let down and, if it's not too fancy a word, unfulfilled. I was still getting offers, but not good ones. Let's face it, if I had been a hot item, I wouldn't have been so hot for home. I had cooled down.

I was "at liberty," as they say in this town when you're out of work, but not for long. Television was just coming into its own then, in the early 1950s, and I was getting a few offers. I did a couple of things without a thought of making any kind of career at it. No one suspected you could have a career on television comparable to one in the movies. No one ever dreamed that TV would top movies.

Early in 1952 Hal Roach, Jr., called to ask if I'd be interested in starring in a summer replacement for "I Love Lucy" called "My Little Margie."

The way it worked in those days, the regular show did thirty-nine weeks, then took thirteen weeks off for summer vacation. The sponsors found a replacement show for the summer, a show they only hoped would be good enough to keep the audience in the habit of tuning in that network at that time during slack season. "I Love Lucy" was on CBS Monday nights from 9 to 9:30, after "Arthur Godfrey's Talent Scouts."

I asked Hal to send over a summary and a script, and Lee and I read it. It was a comedy about a peppy young lady and her rather sedate widowed father. She lived with him and was always getting him or their friends in trouble with her schemes, then had to scheme to get them out. We thought it was pretty good, but we both thought the relationship between father and daughter seemed a little incestuous. Hal said he'd have it rewritten somewhat.

Roach then said he had signed Charlie Farrell to play the father, and since he was still a big name and seemed to suit the part, we liked the idea. Lee thought I should do it, so I decided to. I had little to lose. I was offered $750 a week, which wasn't what I had been making in the movies, but I wasn't making movies anymore, was I? And this was TV. Most movie stars wouldn't do TV at that time.

No one really thought it would pay off. They only ordered nine episodes, rather than the usual thirteen for starters. Now they may order three or four and yank you off after one or two. Then they usually gave you thirteen weeks to see if you could make it. We had only nine. "Arthur Godfrey's Talent Scouts" and Milton Berle's "Texaco Star Theater" were the only shows rated ahead of "Lucy" at the time, so it was a tough act to follow. And summer replacements seldom succeeded, anyway.

The pilot show was called "Reverse Psychology." Margie wanted to talk her dad into doing something, and after reason failed she used reverse psychology by telling him she didn't want him to do it or something like that, and naturally it worked. In those days on a television series the woman was always the clever one who could get the big, good-natured guy to do anything she wanted, one way or another.

The show was panned by the critics—they said it was silly, which maybe it was. But so have been a lot of hits on television, especially situation comedies. "Lucy," for one, was panned as silly by the critics, and it became the biggest hit in the history of television.

I believe that the secret of the success of any sit-com is a combination of things that fall into place. You have to have appealing performers and a chemistry that takes place among them that makes them work well together. You have to have stories that establish the characters and a consistent story line. The stories don't have to be great, but they have to fit the characters, and the characters must have good lines. You have to have good production and a good director who keeps things going. It has to be funny and fast-paced. And then you need a good time slot and opposition you can deal with. If no one tunes in to try you, you can't succeed. In the end, the people like you or they don't. I think there's room for a lot of different things of varying quality on television, but the critics don't seem to realize that the public likes light entertainment better than heavy doses of drama or documentaries, ballet or opera.

We didn't set out to do screen classics. "I Love Lucy" was light, fast, funny, and that was what we wanted our show to be. I was the star, but we had a good cast with Charlie, and with Hillary Brooke, Don Hayden, Clarence Kolb, Willie Best, and Gertrude W. Hoffman. They weren't the biggest names in the business, but you didn't need names on TV; you could create characters, and these people created endearing characters.

George Carlton Brown and Frank Fox gave us fast, funny scripts. And Hal Yates directed us at a fast, funny pace. I had a good feeling about the show from the first because the elements seemed right. We had a great time slot. People were used to tuning into our network at that time. And they continued to do so. The ratings stayed up within reach of what "Lucy" had been getting. The mail was marvelous. And, as so often happens, a lot of critics started to say, Well, it isn't too bad a show after all. (Almost thirty years after it went off the air, I still get fan mail on "My Little Margie," and I am still recognized wherever I go. Some people think my name is Margie.) I never have apologized for the show and never will.

I made my last movie in February and my first episode of "Margie" in April of 1952, so I was certainly not "at liberty" long. We went on the air that June, when the new season started. We were so successful that the sponsors bought the show for the regular season, took us to NBC, and put us on at 7:30 on Saturday nights, which was then prime time.

The sponsors controlled television then. They still do, of course, but not in the same way. Now they almost stand in line for the privilege of sponsorship. But in those days they backed the shows they wanted and bought time on the networks. Today the networks have taken control; they put on the shows they want when they want them, though they still have to sell advertising time. Back in the early 1950s, there was "The Texaco Star Theater," "The Philco-Goodyear Playhouse," and so forth.

Our first sponsor was Philip Morris cigarettes. Stars didn't always do commercials, but Charlie and I did—I liked the idea of a close association with whoever was paying the bills. Neither Charlie nor I smoked, however, so we tossed a coin to see who got smoked out.

Nestlé's tea, Helene Curtis hair spray, and Revlon makeup were some of our other sponsors. If a commercial didn't satisfy the sponsor, we had to do retakes. Doing the hair spray commercial, which required me to look straight at the camera while spraying from the side, I was so determined to avoid retakes that I got so I didn't blink even if some of the stuff landed right in my eye.

All of our sponsors treated us really well. They liked us. They liked our show.

We did so well that they put us on radio, too, which was very unusual, but I didn't want to do it. I was working harder on the television show than I had ever worked in the movies, even in one of those six-day wonders. In fact, among the reasons why Hal Roach, Jr., asked me to do his television shows were that I had worked on the six-day wonders, that I learned my lines well and could do them without one retake after another, that I worked hard and followed direction, that I didn't complain and cause problems, that I was as professional as I could be. I was proud of that record, and worked hard to back it up.

We did thirty-nine new shows a season on television. Years later, they cut back to twenty-six and filled in with reruns. Still later, they cut back some more. Today some series do only thirteen episodes, and there are more reruns than regular shows. The stars now won't work as hard as we did. And they get ten times as much money.

We worked six days a week on the television show. Later, the Screen Actors Guild and AFTRA, protecting performers, cut back to five days a week. We did two shows a week—three days' preparation for each. I had to get up at 5 every morning to dress, grab breakfast, and get to the studio by 6. It took two hours for makeup, most of which time was spent on my hair. That was because we often ended one day making shots of one scene and started the next day making shots of the same scene, and my hair had to match the previous shots.

I have emotional hair that likes to do its own thing, and it often took two strong men to wrestle it back into the way it had been before.

We got an hour off for lunch, but I wouldn't even leave the area. I'd have a sandwich and watch the rushes from the day before. I wanted to keep my characterization on track. I'd watch and catch myself. They wouldn't even let me go to the bathroom until they stopped shooting for a few minutes in order to set up the next shot; then I had to rush or the director would start to shout for me. And usually during these breaks my public relations man, Charlie Pomerantz, was introducing me to some guest on the set or asking me to do an interview with a reporter. They get a lot out of you, I guarantee you. They were always stretching the day's shooting schedule by begging you to go on just another half-hour.

When they approached me to do the radio show, that was more madness. The only way I could have done it would have been to give up sleeping, because there weren't any other hours available to me. Hal Roach said he'd give me a day off to do the radio show. Some day off! Then they offered me 10 percent ownership in both shows. Now that was something that just wasn't done. Lee said it looked like a lifetime annuity, because the show looked as though it would go on forever. I weakened and gave in. Charlie got the same deal. But he was in his fifties and I was only in my thirties. I don't know why he gave in, but I'm sure it was hard on him.

I've never minded hard work. Digging ditches or doing dishes would have been different, but I loved to perform. I never seemed to get tired. On stage, I could go on and on; the adrenalin would pour through me. Then I'd fall into bed exhausted.

I don't want to be overworked. No one does. And I was. But I didn't have to do it. I did it out of a love of the life I was leading. The only time I complained about working too hard was when I didn't like the work I was doing and it got me down and I let down. "My Little Margie" was fun and I was on a high.

9

"My Little Margie" was successful because it was fast and funny and had characters an audience could love. I did not play myself, but I put a lot of myself into my character, Margie Albright. One of the advantages to doing a long-running series is that you can really create a character. The writers get to know you and can write for you and your character. If you will look at the first and the fiftieth show of any successful series, you will see how the key characters have changed and developed.

Despite all my movie experience, I found I still had a lot to learn about television. It's a very intimate medium, and you are very close to the audience. We did 126 episodes of "Margie." They have you under a magnifying glass, and the slightest gesture may appear exaggerated, so you have to keep control of your body and your facial expressions even when you are running amok.

Anyway, basic comedy is built on tragedy. Light tragedy maybe, like someone slipping on a banana peel or getting a pie in the face or walking into a door just as someone pushes it from the other side, which goes back to the French farces of many years ago—but a sort of tragedy, nevertheless. We had a lot of slapstick in "Margie," but some subtleties, too. The comedy came out of the characterizations.

My trademark became a kind of gurgle in my throat; I don't know when it started. I guess it was something I just did. The writers didn't write it in until it was called for; then I'd give it to 'em. Wherever I went, people would ask me to gurgle. It wasn't the classiest of sounds, but everyone loved it. It was just a bit of accidental inventiveness that proved to be popular. It became a part of Margie. And I became Margie every day on the set.

I seemed to have a natural flair for comedy, but I had to learn to time my lines for laughs. Hal Yates kept things going on the screen. He was a wonderful director who knew what would work and what wouldn't. Even something as simple as running into a door when someone opens it will work no matter how many times it is done if it is timed perfectly and surprises people when it happens, but it will not work if it is expected or if it isn't timed properly.

Many in the business agree that comedic acting is much harder than dramatic acting. It may not seem that way but it *is* harder to get a laugh than it is to bring tears. Jack Lemmon tells a story about Edmund Gwenn, the great old character actor. Visited at his bedside as he was dying, Gwenn was asked how hard it was on him. "It's hard, very hard," he said, "but not as hard as doing comedy."

One of the hardest things I had to do on the show was work with animals. It seemed to be my fate to be stuck with them.

The worst was a chimp. Chimps may look lovable, but they can be devils. I was supposed to walk around with this one on my hip, as if he were my baby. Every time we started to shoot a scene he'd reach up and pull the hairs on the back of my neck. I'd tell the trainer, and he'd say "No, no," to the chimp and wag his finger at him. Then we'd start again and the chimp would make sure the trainer wasn't looking, and he'd start to pull the hairs on the back of my neck again. Chimps are so smart.

The chimp would bare his teeth and smile at me in that cute way they have when I was sure he wanted to eat my head. He'd reach around and pinch me under the arm. Hard. I mean it hurt. I told the trainer it hurt. He said, "No, no," and wagged his finger at the animal.

But one day the chimp broke away and ran up onto the catwalk. They had the darnedest time getting him back. The trainer and his wife, who worked with him, took him into a corner of the set and beat him unmercifully. I mean, they just beat him and beat him until he was whimpering terribly. Poor thing! No wonder he was mean! And when they were done, you know what he did? When the lady sat down, he crawled onto her lap and practically cried to be comforted.

After that, I told the writers they could write all the animals into the scripts they wanted, but I wouldn't come within camera range. They didn't have to steal the scenes from me; they could have them.

I did a lot of physical comedy on the show. Prat-falls and all. One time I was suspended from the ceiling, and I thought I was going to strangle. They padded me out until I was twice my size. They rigged a harness. And they gave me helium. I didn't bloat up, but I could hardly breathe while I was being pulled up. I was squealing for real, because helium temporarily takes your voice way up high.

Another time we did a scene where two heavies were chasing me through our apartment. I was supposed to run through the door to the terrace, then try to hold it shut until one of them pushed through it. It wasn't supposed to be a test of strength; it was just to look like it. Obviously I couldn't hold a big man away for long. The door opened toward me so we had to time it and let it open just as he burst through.

The first time we tried it, the door just missed my head. The second time, it *hit* my head. When they shot the scene, the man came through before he was supposed to, and the door hit me in the face and broke my nose. I knew it the minute I was hit. It hurt like heck. And bled that way. They took me to MGM because it was nearby, and the doctor packed my nose to stop the bleeding, but said he couldn't do anything else; it would just have to heal by itself. I was worried that it would mar my perfection, but he said the bone was intact and I would have my pert little schnozz back in no time.

After that, I played in pain. Well, pain builds character.

A far less happy ending came to another scene. We had a show where we were thinking of renting a house when we discover that criminals want something that's in the house. Little Miss Fix-It wants to catch them, so she goes up on the roof and spies on them through the skylight. Only she falls through the glass into the room. Stunt people do this sort of thing all the time. It's not real glass that can cut them; they don't have far to fall, and they land on mattresses off camera. Then the shooting is stopped and the actor takes his place as though he had just landed there and goes on with the scene.

The stunt was set up and the mattresses were placed where the stunt woman was supposed to land. The only thing that worried her was that there was a fairly large metal lip at the edge of the skylight so she couldn't fall straight down; she would have to go over the lip first. They tried to fix it but couldn't. She said it would be all right; she could get over it. They took so long setting it up that I went home. It was the last shot at the end of a long day. The next day I learned that she had broken her back. I felt terrible. Everyone did. But they used that scene.

You don't keep up with the people you work with. There are too many of them from picture to picture, from television show to television show.

I had a stand-in named Babe Kane who was very dear to me. She did a lot of dirty work, like standing under the hot lights for me so my makeup wouldn't be ruined while they set up their camera angles and all. We spent a lot of time together on the set and got to be quite close. I have no idea what happened to her.

Most of the stories centered around Margie trying to keep the ladies away from her father. Right at the top of the show, during the introduction, Margie wondered why she couldn't have a comfortable father instead of such an appealing person. Charles Farrell, who played Vernon Albright, certainly was an appealing person. He was a dear man and we all loved him.

Charlie was in his early fifties when we did the show. He had been born in the Boston area. After he broke into movies he had his biggest success costarring with Janet Gaynor in *Seventh Heaven* in 1927. She won an Oscar, but he didn't. However, he costarred with her in films into the 1930s; they were the leading romantic couple of films at that time. Many people think he married her, but he married another actress, Virginia Valli.

He founded and managed the Palm Springs Racquet Club and made a fortune out of it. The fanciest people in the world vacationed at his tennis layout. By the time he started our show he was serving as mayor of Palm Springs, one of the great resort towns in the world. He made a comeback on our show, not having acted at all for ten years. He was a great-looking person, a distinguished gentleman who was perfect for the part as my silver-haired and slightly helpless father. He had such a childlike quality that I actually always felt older than he.

I wouldn't hurt Charlie for the world, but he knows that what I'm going to say is true. He often tells stories about himself. He was a bit of

71

an absentminded professor and was very nervous about returning to acting. Another performer can sense when one is uptight, and I saw it in Charlie. He always had his script with him, and he was always reading it and trying to memorize his lines between takes. He'd be studying the next scene while we were shooting one and forget his lines for the one we were shooting. We had to hit our marks, and he'd miss them.

I have said Hal Yates was a great director, but on the set he was tough, extremely demanding of everyone and not too patient with anyone. He had a fast temper. When it boiled over, he would start to scream. He was a screamer. That was just his way, and we got used to it. But he landed on Charlie a lot.

We had different actors and actresses from show to show, playing a girl who was going after Charlie or a fellow who was going after me. I was so sensitive to Hal's ways that I would take the guest performers aside and warn them that Hal was a good director but a demanding one who lost his temper a lot and hollered a lot and just to take it in stride, because he was the same with everyone. I remember one actor I had to dance with; I could feel him shaking while he held me after Hal had reached his exasperation point a few times.

Hal's insistence on keeping up a fast pace was such that he did not permit any pauses of any length at all. And Charlie often hesitated. And Hal would holler at Charlie until we all felt sorry for him.

Charlie was the single most considerate man I've ever known in my life. I bled internally for him, but he took the ill treatment in stride. He had no vanity at all. He just loved "Margie"—he never complained to Hal or about Hal and he was happy to be back in the spotlight. Later, he had his own show, and I was happy for *him*.

Gil Stratton, who was on our radio show, tells of vacationing with his wife, Dee, then his fiancée, in Palm Springs and taking her to the Racquet Club to meet Charlie. Gil played my boyfriend, Freddie, on the show, and Charlie always called him Freddie: he could never remember that Freddie was Gil. When Gil arrived with Dee, Charlie greeted him warmly: "Good to see you, Freddie; glad you could come." Gil introduced him to Dee, and Charlie was very gracious to her. When someone stopped by their table, Charlie introduced them: "I want you to meet Freddie Wilson and his girl friend, Gale Storm."

Charlie has told this one on himself. Once when he was sitting with a friend at the club, a man coming in spotted him, waved enthusiastically, and started over. Obviously the man knew Charlie, but Charlie didn't know him. Not wanting to embarrass the man, he desperately asked his companion whether he knew him. He didn't. The man reached Charlie, who jumped up and greeted him warmly. "Good to see you," Charlie said. The man said, "Great to see you, Charlie," then sat down and started to chat. Charlie faked it as best he could, but eventually the man realized that Charlie didn't remember him. "You don't remember me, do you?" he asked. Charlie said, "Oh, sure I do. It's just the name . . ."

The man said, "You don't remember Jackson Hole?"

Relieved, Charlie said, "Oh, sure I do, Mr. Hole."

The man looked at Charlie and said, "Just call me Jackson."

It turned out they had met at Jackson Hole, Wyoming.

Charlie was a dear. So was Clarence Kolb, who played Mr. Honeywell, and Gertrude W. Hoffman, who played Mrs. Odetts.

Clarence was a great old-timer. Because he was hard of hearing, he sometimes misunderstood the director's instructions, and Hal would holler at him.

When Gertrude Hoffman was getting into the business, there was another Gertrude Hoffman who was famous as a stripper, so our Gert added the "W" as her middle initial. We explained to her that no one was going to confuse her with a stripper.

Gertrude was in her eighties, and whenever she had to do anything slightly physical we worried that she would have a heart attack or something. She was a trouper, though, and never failed. She had a problem, too. She didn't live in the real world. Her husband had had a museum in Santa Barbara, and she had gotten into acting late in life. Between scenes she'd come up to me with a script and ask me what this meant or that meant—a slang phrase, for instance. I remember she asked me one time what a hot rod was. When I told her, she was so pleased. She had a sense of discovery about her, as if all of life were an adventure, and it came through on the screen.

Don Hayden, who played Freddie Wilson on the television show, came from an acting family. His mother's maiden name was Bliss and his father's was Hayden, and they ran the Bliss-Hayden

School of Acting for many years. RKO sent many of its young contract players there, and I studied there for a time. They told me I'd be better off without coaching because my personality was so natural that I shouldn't take the chance of stifling it. I am grateful to them for that. Don was very dependable on the set, if not off it. I think he married a different gal every year we were on the show. We couldn't keep track of his wives.

Willie Best, who played Charlie, was a great trouper who'd been around and was a joy to work with.

Hillary Brooke, who played Roberta Townsend, was elegant. She had a wonderful wardrobe. In fact, she once said, when she started in movies, she was hired as much for her clothes as for her ability. She had started at the bottom, in "B's," as I did, and studios often couldn't afford a wardrobe for a star. If she could provide her own costumes, she was in. But Hillary was a beauty who had weathered the years well; she was a professional, and she performed beautifully on our show.

Gil Stratton and Verna Felton, who were the regulars with Charlie and me on our radio show, also were pros.

On radio Gil originated the role Jerry Lewis played in the movie *That's My Boy* as Eddie Mayehoff's son. But from childhood he had always wanted to be a sportscaster, and that's what he became on radio and TV in L.A.

We were happy families—we really were. It would have been pretty tough to do 126 television shows and more than a hundred radio shows together if you didn't get along, but there were not too many big egos involved. Since the stories were different, Charlie and I actually did do more than 126 "Margies." The radio shows were easier. You didn't have to worry about how you looked, and you didn't have the action; and you didn't have the setups and retakes. But you still had to do them. And I was the central figure in every one.

The mistake that was made on "Margie" was that I *was* the central figure in every one of them, especially on television. I used to go to the writers or the director or the producer and suggest that they do some episodes in which Charlie or Don or Hillary or someone else became the center of attention and carried the load for a change, not only to give me a break, but to give the audience a break. They agreed it was a good idea. But when they went to the sponsors, the sponsors said no. They wanted Margie.

That was a mistake. The point I tried to make has been proven over and over again as shows like "All in the Family," "The Mary Tyler Moore Show," "The Bob Newhart Show," "Taxi," and "Barney Miller" have endured by using their ensemble casts almost equally. Sure, there were stars who were the center of attention, but the other characters have carried the story line and the load from episode to episode.

However, three or four years can be a lifetime for a show in show business. Do a show on Broadway for that time and you feel as if you've been doing it forever. Doing "Margie" on television and radio for that time, I felt as if I'd been doing it forever.

I loved "My Little Margie." I loved the character, I loved my co-workers, I loved the show, I loved doing it. I'd get tired, but I'd wake up every morning looking forward to the day's work. I think that the secret to happiness is being surrounded by people you love and having work that you look forward to doing. The show was a success, so we were able to keep on doing it a long time. It made me more of a success than I'd ever really dreamed of.

10

M y Little Margie" opened many doors for me. I did all sorts of
other television shows, played Las Vegas, and made hit records.
In those days, movie and television stars were brought in to
headline Las Vegas shows without any idea of what they could do.
The casinos thought they could build any kind of act around them
and gamblers would be drawn in by the names on the marquees.

They didn't know what I could do, but they offered me $7,500 a
week to do it for four weeks during the summer of 1953. I could have
planned to stand there like a stick and stare at the audience, for all
they knew.

They didn't know I could sing and dance. Once, just to see what it
was like, Lee and I hired Milton Rogers, an arranger-conductor who
also wrote special material, and we put together a real nightclub act. I
worked my fanny off.

Although we had done our radio show before a live audience, I
had never really performed live on my own before and I was scared
half to death, shaking before I went on. Maybe I surprised the
audience. So many "names" had come in and flopped that when I
gave them a real show they loved it, and I was a hit.

As soon as the bosses at the Thunderbird saw what I could do,
they signed me to come back for another four weeks the following
summer, 1954, for another $7,500. I found that I liked performing
before a live audience as much as anything I had ever done.

They loved "Margie" and they loved "Gale" and I loved them for it. But Lee and I didn't really like being in Las Vegas. We didn't like the night life. It was hard for me to do a dinner show at 8 and a drink show at midnight.

There's a hard edge to that town. I can see why so many love it, but it's just not our kind of town. Money is cheap there. Many can afford to blow thousands; many cannot. We got the feeling that lots of people were blowing meal money at the tables and on the slots.

We could have gone back, but we just didn't want to do it anymore. We didn't need it. We took the $60,000 I earned there and built the U-shaped house in Encino in which we lived for about twenty-four years.

We went from a little house on a fifty-foot lot to a large house on an acre of ground. We looked in Beverly Hills because the taxes are lower, but we liked the Valley, and we got a good deal on the property there. We were able to build what we wanted without worrying about a budget.

We even had servants' quarters because we had live-in help to take care of the boys when we were away. It's interesting how easily you can accustom yourself to luxuries in life.

During the run of "Margie" I did more and more television. During our summer replacement period in September of 1952, I did a drama, *The Puppeteers*, on "The Unexpected." In the summer of 1954 I did another, *The Hot Welcome* on "Pitfall."

The best part I ever had was the Claudette Colbert role in the television adaptation of the Orson Welles movie *Tomorrow Is Forever* on "Robert Montgomery Presents," one of the best dramatic anthologies TV has ever had. That was in October of 1955.

I also did a lot of the television variety shows, especially after I started to turn out hit records that I could do on these shows. Usually they'd let me sing whatever new song I had out, but not always. And I often acted in skits.

It was an eye-opening experience.

For instance, I did two or three Perry Como shows. He was on in one way or another for about fifteen years. He seemed an extremely easygoing and nice person.

My first big record hit was "I Hear You Knockin'," which I really liked doing. But I had done it on a previous Como show. So when I was signed to do the show again and found I was scheduled to do "Knockin'," I went to the producer and politely suggested I do my new hit, "Teen Age Prayer," instead. I explained the situation and how it would be better for both the show and me. I thought I had sold him.

He just said, "You'll have to talk to Perry."

When I explained the situation to Perry, he kept saying, "Uh-huh, uh-huh." But when I was finished he just said, "I want you to sing 'I Hear You Knockin'.' " I asked if I could play the new record for him. He nodded. He listened. And he said, "I want you to sing 'I Hear You Knockin'.' "

So that was that.

Milton Berle was the biggest thing on the tube for a while: "Mr. Television." A lovable clown. I was supposed to do two songs on one of his shows. In rehearsal the show ran long, and they decided to cut one of my songs rather than anything of "Uncle Miltie's."

Fair enough, I supposed. He was the star. It didn't matter what the contract called for. I'd get my $2,500 or $3,000 or whatever it was no matter what, though I did want to sing the second song and had counted on the exposure. What bothered me was the way he told me.

He came to my dressing room, which had a waist-to-head mirror running all along one wall. Wearing a towel around his neck, and clad in a silk robe, he came in and paced up and down alongside the mirror while he told me what had been decided.

He never once looked at me. He gazed at his image until he got to the end of the mirror, executed an about-face, and studied himself in the mirror as he came back to the other end, and so on. He'd reach up and touch up his makeup here, his hair there.

He said he was sorry my number had to go, but he was sure I understood that his public watched the show because of him. He gave a deeply dramatic performance. And he left without a glance at me. And without my having gotten in one word.

Bob Hope had an entourage of "yes men" with him wherever he went on the set. He was so surrounded you couldn't get close to him. He is an American institution, of course, our profession's gift to our servicemen, and a living legend. And he didn't treat me badly; he didn't treat me at all. I hardly saw him all week as the show was prepared.

I Ain't Down Yet

We did rehearse a duet on "Silver Bells," to be done in a Christmas setting. A chorus was supposed to start and we were supposed to walk on, arm in arm. But we didn't rehearse our entrance.

During the show, when we were ready to enter, we stood backstage, waiting to go on. I asked him which side I should stand on, which arm he wanted to take. He didn't answer. When the music started, I put an arm through his. He pulled his arm away. Came our cue, he walked out without me. I hurried to catch up, but he'd neither take my arm nor let me take his.

Jack Benny was something else. The first thing I noticed about his show was that during the reading of the script, as we all sat around a table to talk things over at the start of rehearsal, the performers didn't hesitate to say this line didn't sound right or wouldn't it be better to do that thing this way. And Benny talked it over with the performers as if they were real people, and much of the time he agreed with them.

He had no entourage. He even went to the bathroom by himself. He said good morning to everyone when he came on the set and good night to everyone when he left. He wasn't self-centered at all and went out of his way to be nice to everyone. And, maybe because of this, everyone was nice to everyone else on that show. It was the keenest company of stars you could have—Phil Harris, Rochester, Don Wilson, Hy Averback, Mel Blanc.

The song I had to do was "You Make Me Feel So Young." I hadn't recorded it, so I couldn't lip-synch it the way I usually did. I worked hard with the orchestra leader, and I guess Jack could see I was concerned about it. Before the show, when we were standing backstage, I was so worried I was probably shaking. Jack came to me, put his arm around me, and told me, "Don't worry, kid. You're going to be great."

I was not. He was. He was the master of comic character and comic timing. He was also a master of human nature. He was neither cheap nor vain. The character he played was, and he played it beautifully. Remember that show when a gunman sticks him up, saying, "Your money or your life." The long silence starts to draw laughter. The gunman impatiently repeats his request. "I'm thinking, I'm thinking," Benny says.

He once told this one on himself. He said it really happened to him:

Leaving a hotel with his agent on the way to the airport, Benny stopped to use a lobby bathroom, then hurried into a cab. Pulling away, Benny realized he didn't have his wallet and decided it must have dropped from his pocket while he was sitting on the throne. They were late, but Benny insisted they return so he could retrieve his wallet. Rushing into the bathroom, he bent down and saw his wallet lying way back in the stall. It was a pay toilet, and Jack of course didn't have any change. Desperate, he bent back down and crawled as far under the door as he could, reaching for the wallet. At that moment someone entered and saw what appeared to be a man sneaking under the door to get into the pay toilet without paying. When Jack heard him he straightened up and turned around, and the man saw that it was that notorious tightwad Jack Benny—living up to his stage and screen character in real life.

Jack was one of the sweetest men I've met in a business not notorious for sweet men, and I miss him very much.

Randy Wood was sweet, too. My recording career was with his Dot Records. Randy lived in Gallatin, Tennessee. He was at home one time when his daughter Linda, who was about twelve, saw me guesting on Gordon McRae's television show. She called her dad in to see "My Little Margie" singing.

He phoned me to ask if I'd like to try recording. I was thrilled at the thought but put Lee on to talk to him. Randy was a charmer who could sell anyone anything on the telephone, and Lee liked him and liked the idea. But when Lee asked about terms, Randy wondered whether we might take stock in the company. Lee worked out a royalty deal instead.

Lee hadn't heard of the company. I hadn't, either. Randy had signed Pat Boone and some others, but he hadn't had any hits yet. We thought we were wise to play it cautious. We weren't. I made a lot of money out of my recordings. I sold six million records. I had one gold record which sold a million copies. Altogether, I made maybe $100,000 in royalties. Randy's company became one of the biggest before it was sold to Gulf & Western, and my stock in it would have been worth many times what I made in royalties.

However, it was great for me—a real learning experience, and I just loved it.

I went to Chicago in the fall of 1955, right after "Margie" went off the air, for my first recording session with Dot Records. I had prerecorded songs for movies, but this was a bit different. The emphasis was on the recorded sound, not on how I would appear singing on a screen.

Randy knew his stuff. Like many directors he was kind, but firm. Since I was new at this, I did what I was told. If I was right, the orchestra wasn't. Or the sound level wasn't. We did retake after retake until Randy was satisfied.

I suppose any work that is worthwhile is hard.

Mostly, I "covered" records that were hits or looked as if they were going to be. Today the critics look down on rock stars who don't write their own songs or who record the hits of others, but yesterday it was common practice. The songs were on the Hit Parade, not the star's record. If Crosby had a hit, Como, Sinatra, Haymes, Dinah Shore and others recorded the same song. Sometimes the second or third record became the big one.

Frequently I had to listen to the original record to get the words right. We mostly used our own arrangements, but we also copied a lot of these, too. It seemed so sneaky, but for a while I was in no position to protest. They said everyone did it, and I guess everyone did. But when I did "Dark Moon" I did protest, because Bonnie Guitar had not only written it but recorded it, and I liked her record. They insisted she'd be happy even if my record was a bigger hit than hers, because as the songwriter she'd make that much more money. But I didn't believe them and refused to do it unless she gave me permission herself. By golly, they brought her to the studio and she *did* give it to me.

After a while they began to bring me new stuff, too, and that was a thrill for me. And an even bigger thrill when top singers began to cover my records. I tried not to copy other singers but rather to sing each song as I felt it, and I did develop a style of my own, which I can hear when I listen to my old records. But I'm sure I unconsciously copied the originals at first.

My first, "I Hear You Knockin'," was a cover of something someone named Smiley Louis, the rhythm-and-blues man, had done. I don't think it had become a hit yet, but it promised to be one. It was a real rock-and-roll song, but then of course this was the rock-and-roll era. My copy came out in October of 1955. I have the

Billboard list of every singer's top one hundred records—records that reached what they call the charts—and this one lasted twenty-one weeks on the charts and reached number two. I know for a fact that it was number one on some other lists.

These were 45-rpm records, the small records that were so big in those days. This was my first gold record. Randy and his associates were thrilled. They hadn't been sure how well I could sing or how well I would do when they signed me, and they were really surprised by how well the record did. In fact, I think it was their first gold record.

I only recorded for eighteen months, and I had ten more records in the top one hundred, three more in the top ten. For me, it was one solid seller after another. "Tell Me Why" came out in June, "Now Is the Hour" and "A Heart Without a Sweetheart" in September, and "On Treasure Island" and "Lucky Lips" the following March, and all reached the charts and lasted for a fair amount of time. "Dark Moon," which came out in April of 1957, was not a gold record, but it reached number five and lasted twenty-three weeks, longer than any of my others.

Trick recordings were used to some extent. I did a duet with myself on "A Heart Without a Sweetheart." Actually I was a trio, since I was pregnant at the time.

11

While I was working with Randy Wood, I started a new television series, "Oh! Susanna." Every third show was a musical. Randy saw to it that I did many of my records on these shows, which promoted the records. Randy always knew his own mind, and it was difficult to argue with him. I might want to do this song or that song this way or that way, but even after I had established myself as a pop star, we did what Randy wanted done—his way.

He also was an extremely attractive man. Lee saw this. Randy loved his wife and I loved Lee. I told Lee this many times, but he was always concerned. I regularly flew to Chicago to record at Bill Putnam's studio, which Randy used. Lee frequently went with me, but sometimes his business prevented him from going. He'd call me all the time: "Where's Randy? Is Randy there?" Randy was usually there.

Recording, you spend long hours in the studio. Randy and I would break for a bit of lunch or dinner. Sometimes we'd relax with a drink. We were both away from home for a few days, and we were together all the time. I suppose he also spent time with the other performers when he was recording with them. Still, Lee didn't like it.

Neither Lee nor I knew anything about the music business. I was learning as I went, but Lee wasn't involved in it. It was the first time he had no knowledge of my business at all. Television was just another form of movies; so was radio. But not recording. Randy and I became so close and were together so constantly that it was hard for Lee not to become jealous of him. Lee will tell you this also. He wants me to tell the story because it's the truth; it affected my career, and it's an important part of my story.

No matter how many times I told Lee that nothing was going on between Randy and me, he just wasn't satisfied. My recording career was really important to me, and I could see it was threatened by his jealousy. We really love each other, but at that time we were both a little insecure, and on guard against anything that threatened our marriage.

I didn't want to leave Randy and my recording career. But I didn't want to lose Lee, either. And we were having awful arguments. I didn't know where to turn. So I went to see Cleveland Kleihauer, the minister at the church we were attending at the time. I wept and poured my heart out to him. I got Lee to go with me to see him. Counseling has helped us several times in our lives, but it was no help then.

It got to the point where I had to tell Randy I couldn't record in Chicago anymore. He arranged to record me in L.A. But before something went out of my relationship with Lee that could never be replaced, I quit Randy and recording. I didn't sign with another company, though I could have.

I loved everything about the business—learning new songs, developing a style, going into the studio, working with backup singers and an orchestra, getting a recording right, hearing it on the radio, seeing it succeed, knowing I was a successful singer. It was an enormously exciting experience that sends shivers down my spine when I think about it.

But the one thing that always meant more to me than movies or music or anything was my husband and family. I don't feel that bad about giving up anything for Lee, because I know he'd give up anything for me.

If music was a great experience for me, we both benefited from the bad experience that went with it. Without trust in a marriage, there isn't much. The lives of married people are so intimately intertwined that if you aren't completely comfortable with one another, can't confide in one another, don't communicate well with one another, it won't last.

I don't think it comes easy. It takes time and effort. You have to learn as you go along. If you can get through the rough times, you can make your marriage a good one. Lee and I learned not to let jealousy spoil our marriage.

What the heck, most of us are exposed to temptation at one time or another. It's hard to resist sometimes, too. And it's hard to be forgiving. For a while I found fault with everything Lee did. But I truly believe love can conquer all. If a couple really cares about one another, they are understanding. If I hadn't been understanding of Lee's jealousy, perhaps he wouldn't have understood my alcoholism later. And if we hadn't had some rough times in our forty years of marriage, we wouldn't have been human.

We've had our fights—hollering at one another, once in a while throwing something. Both of us believe the best of us need educated counseling from time to time. In fact, Lee helped set up a counseling service at Bel-Air Presbyterian. I've seen psychiatrists and psychologists. It's an inexact "science," and a bad professional can do harm, but if you can find a good one, he can help.

You may conclude that such problems as we had contributed to my alcoholism, but I cannot. I'm talking about forty years of marriage. I'm dealing with the highlights . . . or the low lights. I figure we had fewer problems than most people. Our love never wavered. Our feelings for family never wavered. Our faith never wavered.

With Lee and me both working, we did not give our sons as much time as we would have liked, but we treasured our time with them and gave them as much love as we had in us. Phillip, Peter, and Paul had their problems, like any kids, but I think they grew up normally well adjusted. They were not impressed that their mother was a celebrity. Because we lived in the Valley and not in Beverly Hills or Newport Beach, they did not grow up among stars. They had some luxuries, but no more than their friends. We tried not to spoil them.

There was a time when Pete got into a little trouble, and it was blown all out of proportion because his mother was well known. This was later on:

He and some friends had enlisted in the Marines and went on a beer bust to celebrate. They were driving around in Pete's camper and decided to go see a girl they knew in Encino. They were getting hungry, and they passed an elementary school where they knew there was food in the kitchen. Pete didn't even go in, but the others forced their way in and took some Jell-O out to the camper to eat. That's all they took.

The police came along and arrested them. Somehow the press got wind of it, and the radio and television and newspapers reported that Gale Storm's son Peter "and three friends" had been arrested on the charge of breaking and entering. We found out about it when a friend called up to tell us she'd heard it on the radio.

It was wrong of them to do it, but it was the sort of thing young people did. We stood by our son, and charges were dismissed the same day. But as usual the newspapers gave this a lot less space than they had given the original report. And they never did mention the other boys by name, only "Gale Storm's son, Peter Bonnell." It hurt because I had brought this on him almost as much as he had brought it on himself. If it had not been for me, he would not have received nearly so much attention.

It still hurts because a few people still vaguely remember Pete as having been in some kind of trouble as a young man—as if he had been an armed robber or a drug pusher or some such thing. Pete had always been steady and conservative. As the oldest of the boys, Phil may have been pushed hard. Lee was extremely proud and demanding of his sons. He wanted them to do well. He meant well, but I worried that his standards were too high. From the time I turned over management of my career to him, he made decisions for me. Later, when I started to drink heavily, he ran the family.

We almost lost Phil one time. Lee and I had gone to Mexico City on a vacation in 1962 when we got a call from my sister-in-law telling us that Phil had been seriously injured in an automobile accident and that the doctors needed our permission to operate. We were told he was in a coma with a fifty-fifty chance of survival. We gave permission, then almost went mad before we could get a plane out the next morning.

At the hospital, the doctor told us it might be a week or ten days before Phil even came out of his coma. He had severe head injuries, and was so bandaged that we could see only his mouth.

But when we took his hands and spoke to him, he wasn't in a coma after all. He stunned us by saying, "Hi, Mom. Hi, Dad. I'm sorry I spoiled your vacation."

We wept and we prayed. And we were heard. Phil was out of the hospital within a week. He still needed plastic surgery, but he came out of it okay. It caused him to miss a year of college.

You cannot count on your kids to go through life without problems, sickness, or injury; you do what you can, and you pray for them. Phil, Peter, and Paul survived their childhoods and are out in the world doing well. So is Susie, born in 1956 and named after "Oh! Susanna."

In 1957, we bought a boat so we could take the boys water-skiing. I went for a swim one day when the water was rough. Lee tried to pull me back into the boat; I swung to the side and cracked my hip against the boat and wrenched my back. Later I suffered really bad back pain. My left leg ached terribly. I was in agony.

"Oh! Susanna" was a physical show in which I had to run and jump and dance. Now I just couldn't do it—but I did anyway. For almost a year I went from doctor to doctor—orthopedic surgeons, mainly—without satisfaction. They agreed I had ruptured a disc in my lower back and it was pinching the sciatic nerve, but none of them were themselves sufficiently confident of successful surgery to inspire my confidence in them. Finally my makeup man, Tom Case, hesitantly recommended a doctor who had developed a new technique and had performed successful surgery for a similar condition on his mother-in-law.

This doctor turned out to be a bronzed god, a powerful former Olympic swimmer, a tall, dark and handsome devil who had confidence in himself and inspired a remarkable amount of confidence in me.

In the normal operations for ruptured discs at that time, the disc was removed and was replaced with small pieces of bone cut from elsewhere in your body. My new doctor was ahead of his time. He took whole bone from another part of the body and fused the spine with it by wedging it into place permanently. He took the graft from the sacral bone, where your rear cheeks dimple, an area where bone is not desperately needed.

The surgery on me was successful—though I no longer have a dimpled behind.

12

I had worked so hard on "My Little Margie" that I vowed I would not do another television series unless it was something I absolutely couldn't resist. I might do another movie. I could do theater. I was making records. But I was not going to get involved in another television series.

"Margie" had been off the air less than one year and had gone into reruns in syndication when Lee Carson, who had been one of the best writers on the Margie show, called my husband to say he had an idea for a new series he wanted to write for me. Lee told him there was no chance whatsoever I'd do it, but I'd be happy to talk with him about it.

When I met with him, right off I told him there was no chance whatsoever I would do another series. What I didn't reckon with was the elaborate proposal he had put together. It consisted of the back page of a *Time* magazine, with a color picture of a cruise ship. It was an advertisement for luxury cruises. It mentioned that the cruises had a social director to keep the guests entertained. He wanted me to play a social director on a cruise ship. That was it. That was the entire proposal.

To me, a cruise on a ship seemed like the ultimate luxury. The movies that had been made about life at sea on cruise ships made it all seem very romantic. As we talked, we could envision the colorful characters who would take cruises. And the madcap antics this former "Margie" could get into and out of as social director on such a ship. Without a line of script, I was sold.

Carson took his elaborate proposal to Hal Roach, Jr., and, with me as the possible star but without a line of script, Hal bought it. Since I was recording and my musical career was booming, Carson came up with the idea that we do every third show in musical variety format. After that, he couldn't have beaten me off with a paddle.

It didn't hurt, either, when he came up with an offer of $3,000 a show and 10 percent of the show. We were still shooting the pilot when the Nestlé company bought it. To sell a show to a sponsor before that sponsor had even seen the pilot was unheard of. We were ecstatic.

We had a half-hour. We had a tie-in with the American Presidents line, but we never went to sea, not once. In fact we never left the Hal Roach Studios lot, where "Margie" had also been shot. They worked the background stuff wonderfully well, so you couldn't tell we weren't at sea.

We had a small standing cast. There was Roy Roberts as Captain Huxley, and ZaSu Pitts as my friend Esmerelda. Jimmy Fairfax played Cedric for three years, but the character was dropped in our fourth and final year.

Our "ship" was the U.S.S. *Ocean Queen*. I had to carry the show. They came up with the name Susanna Pomeroy for me so they could use the subtitle "Oh! Susanna," and that was the title they used in syndication later, but the original show was titled "The Gale Storm Show: Oh! Susanna" so they could capitalize on my fame from "My Little Margie." And we did last four full seasons, which was longer than "My Little Margie."

We were as successful with the second show as we had been with the first, and we were far more stable. We had a little more flexible format on "Susanna" than we'd had on "Margie" and were able to do more varied things, which helped, but I was still in almost every scene. The unions had cut the work week back from six to five days, but I was still leaving home at 6 and getting back at 9, Monday through Friday.

I don't know why I'm not as well remembered for "Susanna" as for "Margie," but I'm not. Almost anyone over the age of thirty remembers Margie, but many do not remember Susanna. Maybe because Margie was first. Maybe because Margie was a more endearing character. Maybe Margie was a better show. It was funnier. But Susanna was fun and it had music—I'd like to be remembered as Susanna as well as Margie.

The pilot show for "Oh! Susanna" was a musical in which I danced in a production number; I'd done it before. Although I'd never had a lesson in my life, I loved it. I didn't know how to do lifts, but I did lifts. You know, one or two big male dancers grab you and hoist you aloft and you lie horizontally on their hands with your legs crossed while they spin you and toss you around and stuff. Ignorance is bliss. I'd have let one of those lifters throw me down a flight of stairs, believing there'd be another one at the bottom to catch me. Well, I did one in which I was spun during a number for the first "Oh! Susanna," but when they put me down I felt dizzy and sick to my stomach. This had never happened to me before. When I told Lee, he took me to my doctor. I was pregnant.

If you have never seen a producer die over lunch at Romanoff's, you should have been with me when I announced my forthcoming blessed event to Hal Roach. We were at this famous restaurant when I made my infamous revelation. He turned pale, and started to strangle on his food. He pushed his plate away. So what if I was going to have a baby? So what if the show depended on me? So what if the show was signed by a sponsor, assigned a time slot, shooting the first episode? He only had about a hundred people assigned to the show in one capacity or another. He didn't have more than a million dollars at stake. I tried to explain that I hadn't planned it this way. It had been nearly ten years since my last one.

I had never even come close to miscarrying with my previous babies so, although I was in my mid thirties, my obstetrician assured me I could continue to work without risk to the infant, for a while at least. I told him I had to jump off a roof and land on my belly in the next day's shooting. He said Fine, go ahead.

I told Hal we could continue to shoot as long as my condition didn't show. I was sure we could fulfill our obligation to the sponsor, getting enough new episodes in the can so that reruns wouldn't be necessary.

Hal agreed to go ahead with me. There was never a mention of a replacement. I don't think they thought of it. I was the show. But they could have canceled it. We had to get an OK from the sponsor. Nestlé's gave us the go-ahead. They went to the wire with me, at great risk, and I will never forget them for it.

We decided to shoot as many episodes as we could as fast as we could. Fortunately we were in a period of full, flaring skirts and petticoats, which concealed my pregnancy. I watched my diet carefully, and the only weight I gained was the baby's. I did a minimum of dances and lifts, and I felt fine. But I can remember shooting one scene standing at the ship's rail and glancing down and seeing my dress move as the baby kicked. I blew my lines that time. But we got through it.

I nearly didn't complete my role as Susanna Pomeroy, but Susanna Bonnell was born the 12th of November, 1956. I was out only a few weeks, and we had a new show to ready each week. Susie made the year especially memorable.

The producer made me swear off sex for the remainder of the series. I told him I had sworn off, but Lee hadn't. We only kidded about these things off camera. Both Susanna and Margie were sexy enough, but these were clean shows without all the double-entendres that mar so many sit-coms these days.

I'm all for sex in its place, and it doesn't embarrass me to talk about it one bit, but I really don't like those series they have today where the characters are bodies, not people, and the stories center on the bedroom and bathroom, and the lines are suggestive, not inventive. Nor do I like the harsh language, open nudity, and intimate sex in movies today. I'm sort of old-fashioned, I suppose; but simply because old values are old doesn't make them wrong.

As with Margie, Susanna schemed to solve people's problems, then had to scheme to solve the problems she created. But she was more mature as a personality.

Her best friend on the ship was Esmerelda Nugent—"Nugey"— her roommate and the ship's beautician, played by ZaSu Pitts. If you remember ZaSu, she was one of those women who must have looked sixty when she was sixteen. She always looked the same and always played scatterbrained characters. She always looked bewildered as she waved enormous hankies around and said, "Oh my, oh my." I used to tell her that if she stole one more scene from me by waving those hankies in front of my face, I was going to start picking my nose on camera whenever she had lines to speak; then she'd get flustered and apologetic.

She was a dear lady who looked frail but had the strength of a horse. If we had three days off, she did another show or campaigned for a political candidate. She hated Democrats and loved Republicans.

ZaSu was pure and dear. She was close to sixty when she did our show and died at sixty-five.

Roy Roberts played stuffy Captain Huxley, who was bedeviled by Susanna. He always played formal figures of authority in the many movies he made, but he could make them funny, as he did in a "Margie" episode. He could play a wide variety of characters, and we had him back often. I suggested him for the part of the ship's captain, and I was delighted when he got it. He was a perfect foil for Susanna.

Jimmy Fairfax was also perfect for Cedric. He was veddy, veddy British, as was the part.

In "Susanna," I doubled in a lot of different parts. I'd be made up to look different; I'd have to act different; and usually I had to use an accent of one sort or another. I played Hollywood stars and southern belles, countesses and businesswomen.

I did a lot of physical things, too. I never got a broken nose, but I almost drowned. In one show Roy and I were supposed to be diving for sunken treasure. In the basic scenes, we were shot from behind a tank of fake underseas, and it looked as if we were underwater. Then we had to do one scene in the tank.

We had on underwater diving equipment, but it wasn't real. The real stuff was too heavy; and, besides, we didn't know how to use it. So we faked it. We had on diving masks with the glass "windows" removed so that we could breathe, but as soon as they started shooting I discovered that someone had forgotten to take the glass out of my mask, and within seconds I simply couldn't breathe. I almost exploded before they waved Roy and me out of the tank.

We did every third show as a musical, usually centered on a ship's party. I was the entertainment director. Our shows were choreographed extensively at a fair cost and came across really well. I enjoyed dancing and singing.

Two years after the show started—it lasted four and a half years altogether—Jack Wrather bought it from Hal Roach, Jr., thank God. Jack sold it later for two and a half million dollars for reruns, for two years only.

Jack, who was married to Bonita Granville, also owned the

Muzak Corporation and the "Lassie" and "Lone Ranger" television series. Jack and Bonita are super people who always gave us a clear accounting of the dollars involved. Over seven years or so, I made pretty good money, though it was hardly big dollars by the standards of today's television stars.

In syndication, as "Margie" had been, "Susanna" was on many, many stations across the country. I think one or the other has been on somewhere even in recent years and may be on somewhere now for all I know.

13

All the bright lights do not blink on Broadway. There is a lot of live theater all across the country—summer theater, year-round theater, theater in the round, and dinner theater. I've done them all with a great deal of satisfaction.

Instead of playing to millions in an unseen television audience, I'd play to hundreds in a real live theater, but I'd get a real live reaction from them, too. Instead of playing one or two characters like "Margie" and "Susanna," I played a dozen or so, all different. Each show was totally different from the others. Each was a good show that had been a hit on Broadway. I never got to play Broadway, but I got to play big cities and suburban towns and country towns in every section of the country.

It was hard work, but there is a connection between a live actor and a live audience that is electric—more thrilling for the actor, I think, than any other kind of performance. I'd be absolutely exhausted at the end of each night's show, but unless it was a bad night I'd also feel a satisfaction I had seldom felt before.

I'd go back to an empty motel room or hotel room or rented apartment late at night and fall into bed. I'd be bored silly during the day, unless Lee was with me. He came with me as often as he could.

At one time Phil wanted to be an actor, and he came to be with me from time to time. Once he worked with me. Other times, Peter or Paul came. More recently, Susie was old enough to come to be with me a while. But most of the time I was alone out there, on my own. I'd play six weeks or more here and there. I was away from home and family more than I liked. But, as I have said, I relished the work. And the money was good.

Before I even did my first television series, I did the comedy *Gramercy Ghost* with the late William Eythe, a lovely man, for a week in St. Louis. Lee wasn't able to come with me, but here's part of a letter from him that was delivered to me at my hotel just before I went to the theater for opening night:

January 1952

My darling,

Since I can't be there tonite on this big occasion, I want you to read this just before you go on stage and know that I'll be thinking of you for the next two hours and pulling for you like I've never pulled before.

Tonite you're going to step on that stage and make a girl named "Nancy" so realistic that the audience won't be able to believe it's just a play. Each line, each move, each piece of business will fall right into place and so will the laughs and after it's over you'll be a polished performer. This play tonite will make you know what a really fine actress you are. You may have doubted it before, but tonite will tell you what I've told you for years—you're just great in comedy. St. Louis will love you. . . .

Of course I telephoned Lee later, and he still has the letter I wrote to him afterwards:

As you can see, the review is very nice . . . I guess I didn't sound very good about the play over the phone, did I? I'm sorry I didn't. I was almost too tired and wrung out to make sense, much less be enthused. However, I felt better when I joined the company downstairs and the director talked to me. He asked me how I felt and I said I was surprised because I expected to feel some great elation or something when I finished, but I didn't.

Then he said, "But my dear, don't you know that you are exhausted, because what you are doing is the most difficult thing there is to do in the theatre?" He went on to say that there were only a few women who could play an ingenue well and that none of them remotely looked like one and that a real ingenue, a young girl, could never do it well and that I was the only one he knew who was so young, who looked so young, who could do it. Whew!! Then he said there is absolutely no doubt but that "it would still be running in New York if you had been playing it." This all sounds quite important when it's written down, but actually it was just tossed off. Anyhow it made me feel better. I'm sure I needed a pat on the back.

After "Margie" ended its television run, I did *Wish You Were Here* at the Texas State Fair in Dallas. I was putting on my act at the Thunderbird in Las Vegas and starting to cut pop records when I got the only opportunity I've ever had to do opera, bringing my lyric soprano to the role of Letitia in Gian Carlo Menotti's *The Old Maid and the Thief* at the Los Angeles Conservatory of Music. It was a genuine thrill.

After "Susanna" ended its TV first run, I did six weeks in *Wildcat* on the Midwest tent circuit, and that really got me going. The show was not the best one I ever did; the book was full of holes, but it worked. The following year I returned to that straw-hat tour through Ohio and other states in *Finians Rainbow*.

Early in 1967 I played *Grand Prize* for five weeks at the Pheasant Run Playhouse in St. Charles, Illinois. Later that year I played Nurse Nellie Forbush and "washed that man right out of my hair" every night for four weeks at the Meadowbrook Dinner Theater in New Jersey, just outside New York.

In 1970 I returned to the theater, the Kenley Star Theatre in Wichita, Kansas, to do my beloved *The Unsinkable Molly Brown*. I did it at the University of Mississippi later in the year, too. Clearly, I wasn't down. I enjoyed doing this Meredith Willson show as much as any I ever did.

I also loved *Cactus Flower*, which I did in 1971 and 1972 in Fort Worth, Dallas, Pineallas Park, Florida, and Hartford, Connecticut. A few years later I played it for long runs in Salt Lake City and then St. Petersburg.

Back in 1971, late in the year, I did the three female leads in Neil Simon's marvelous *Plaza Suite* in Lubbock, Texas, and then in El Paso.

I Ain't Down Yet

In the summer of 1972 I played *Marriage Go-Round* in Denver. From November of 1972 through January of 1973 I had my longest single run, ten weeks, in *Rainy Day in Newark* at the famous Drury Lane Theatre in Chicago.

Aside from *Cactus Flower*, the show I did most often was *Forty Carats*. I played an older woman in love with a younger man. I like love scenes. So does Lee—who often coached my leading men.

A funny thing happened once when I was playing in *Forty Carats* in Denver:

There's a scene near the end in which the gal's ex-husband drops in unexpectedly to see their daughter. The ex-wife is expecting her young lover. Her ex-husband makes them drinks and smokes a cigar while talking to her. When there is a knock at the door, she makes her ex hide in the bedroom as if she doesn't want her lover to know he's been there. But she really does, and after her ex goes to hide, she picks up his cigar and puffs it mightily to fill the room with the strong, smoky smell before her lover enters.

In the scene, the actor starts to leave, spies the two glasses, and returns to scoop them up and take them with him as he goes to hide, leaving his cigar burning in the ashtray by accident. But this one time, as he scooped up the glasses, he caught the cigar between them accidentally and left with it. I spotted the cigar between the glasses as he was going and started to panic. Without the cigar smoke, the scene wouldn't play. But I just waved my hand through the air as if fanning the smoke he'd left behind. When the young man came in and sniffed the air, the audience accepted it.

There are things such as this that happen in live theater you'd never see on the screen.

The only night I ever missed a show, I had a strep throat and—with no voice—couldn't make it through *Finians Rainbow*. That shook me a little, because I always figured I could muddle through somehow. But you don't very often lip-synch your songs to recordings in the theater, and I never did.

The worst time I had was when I was playing *Cactus Flower* at Pineallas Park in Florida.

Paul flew in to be with me for a few days, then flew back home. The airport was in Tampa, about forty-five minutes away, and I drove him there in a rental car early the morning after doing a performance the previous night. I was exhausted, driving back in a bit of a daze, when I ran right into a car in front of me which had been stopped for a red light. I really rear-ended him hard and smashed my face into the steering wheel.

No one was seriously hurt, and the man whose car I hit recognized me and was so excited to meet me that it didn't seem to matter how we'd met. I guess I made his day. He got tickets for the show and everything. He was a former fighter, and when he took a look at my face, he warned me I was going to have a horrible shiner on one eye. I was afraid to look and started to worry about doing the show that night.

He said ice was the best thing for the bruises and actually went into a nearby restaurant to get me crushed ice in a napkin to hold to the side of my face. The cops came and treated me like a criminal. The gentleman who had suffered most of the damage kept apologizing, saying our insurance would take care of everything and didn't they know who I was and obviously I was a responsible citizen. Anyway, I got away without paying.

The minute I got back to my room, I looked in a mirror and saw that one side of my face was turning black and blue, green and red. My eye was swelling shut. I called the producer, and asked him to make an announcement beforehand that I'd had an accident.

They sent a doctor, and he mended me as best he could. Before the show, they sent a makeup man who covered my bruises as best he could. I went on, then, even though one eye was shut tight.

I had not had a drink the morning of that accident. I was not drunk. I just had an accident. But I had begun to drink by that time, rather heavily, in fact.

The last play I did was done on leave from a hospital at which I was being treated for alcoholism. I had signed to do *Cactus Flower* at the Glendale Community College Playhouse outside of Phoenix in March of 1978. I wanted desperately to do it, and I did. But, as many times as I had done the show, I had terrible trouble remembering my lines in rehearsal. The others didn't know what was wrong with me. Lee had to fly in to help me, and it was the worst time of my career. We said I wasn't feeling well, and they went along with me. I got my act together and performed effectively. They were relieved. I wasn't. At this point I could no longer count on being able to perform. At this point I could no longer count on living much longer.

14

I had been blessed in my life. I had a husband I loved and a truly happy marriage. We had four healthy children of whom we were proud. We had a handsome home and enjoyed a good life. We were secure and could look forward to the future without fear. We were relatively healthy and active. You cannot use the usual reasons when you try to figure out why I started drinking heavily. As I said before, there was no tragedy—and not even that much trauma—in my life.

I didn't realize that my body was developing a need for alcohol. I started to have a few drinks at night before I went to bed because I wanted them the way someone with a "sweet tooth" wants candy. Straight vodka. Then I started to have a few drinks during the day. I didn't see anything so wrong with this. When Lee started to notice how much I was starting to drink and tried to talk to me about it, I grew defensive. I didn't want to talk about it. I didn't want to think about it. It was silly. So I had a few drinks; so what?

By the early 1970s our three sons were in their twenties, grown up and gone from home. Our daughter was a teen-ager, too young, I thought, to make much of my drinking. She did start to leave literature around that discussed what people should do if they had a drinking problem, but that only annoyed me, because I didn't think I had a drinking problem. Yet day by day I was drinking more and more and admitting it less and less. Before long my days—and my nights—were dominated by drinking.

By the middle 1970s I was hiding bottles around the house and getting up in the middle of the night to drink and waking up in the morning to have a drink before breakfast. Sometimes I skipped breakfast. And lunch. Vodka has calories, and I was drinking a quart a day and starting to put on weight.

I became careful not to drink before a show or an interview. I was sober on stage because I knew I could drink when I got back home. In this way, I thought I was handling it. Alcoholism could happen to other people, but not to me. I looked forward to leaving home and going on the road to do a show because I could drink more freely when I was alone in my room, without the family around.

When I was home, I tried not to let Lee see how much I was drinking. I drank from different bottles than the ones he'd checked. He knew what I was doing, but I pretended I didn't know he knew. I wouldn't talk to him about it. I'd leave the room. I left all the decisions of my life and our life to him. If he said we were going to someone's house for dinner or someplace for a vacation, we went. If he said I should do this show or that show, I did it. I left everything to him because I didn't want to be bothered, because I was concerned only with drinking and seeing that the world didn't see how much I was drinking. If he had told anyone I had a drinking problem, I would have died. By then I knew. By then I had started to dislike myself. I was doing something I didn't want to do, but I didn't want to stop.

I was not driven to drink by desperation; I was driven to desperation by drink. Lee was terribly concerned, but he is a very kind man and couldn't bring himself to say much to me. By then, I was saying more to myself than anyone could have said to me. It didn't stop me.

For some time I had been searching the mirror for signs that my drinking was affecting me physically, but for a long time I didn't see anything. Apparently my body absorbed the alcohol without trouble for a long time. Suddenly, however, over a period of only about six months, I started to put on weight. My face began to blow up and I looked as if I were six months pregnant.

I had to stop wearing slacks because they wouldn't stretch enough. I shopped for bigger and bigger dresses; eventually I was buying tents to conceal my body. I had taken such pride for so long in my slim figure that it really hurt when I lost it and I couldn't stand to look at myself in the mirror.

Still, this was only one of the last straws. Lee suggested that if I just stopped for a few days I might start to lose weight; but, much as I wanted to, I still couldn't stop drinking. I was ashamed of my appearance, but I was even more ashamed of my character, of my inability to use willpower to stop doing something that was destroying me.

I felt that my husband and my children had to be as ashamed of me as I was of myself. I was a mental wreck. And I was starting to feel terrible physically. I felt drugged. I had no energy. No enthusiasm for anything.

With Lee's encouragement I gave in and decided to see my doctor. Previously, when he'd asked me how much I drank, I'd said I just had a couple of cocktails before dinner or something like that. This time, I admitted I might be drinking a little too much. He knew it. He could see it. He suspected I had a seriously enlarged liver and encouraged me to go to the UCLA Medical Center to see how bad it was.

He also told me I was only kidding myself if I couldn't see for myself how serious it was. He said I appeared to be an alcoholic and if I didn't get off the bottle I'd be getting off the earth. I hated him for saying that to me. I was insulted by it. All right, I had a problem, but I certainly wasn't an alcoholic, I told Lee.

Lee's solution was to pray for me and ask me to pray with him to seek help for me. I didn't want to pray for myself, but I did it for Lee's sake. I never lost faith in God. I never blamed Him for my problems. Still, I didn't understand why I was doing this to myself. But I held Lee's hand, and we prayed for help in the early hours of the day, morning after morning. I know now He was listening to us.

I agreed to check into the UCLA Medical Center to have tests taken. I hoped they might find out there that it was all a mistake and that I had an overactive thyroid gland or something and all I had to do to get back in shape was take some pills, watch my diet, and maybe cut down on my drinking.

We decided to wait until after we had Thanksgiving dinner with the kids. It was terrific to be together. We had by then talked a little from time to time about my drinking and I admitted now that I was having physical problems, but I said I didn't think they were too serious.

They could see for themselves, of course. And they were happy when I told them I was going into the UCLA Center for tests. They were relieved that I was starting to do something about myself. I said we all knew I'd been drinking too much and I was going to give it up. When I said it, I meant it.

Suddenly it seemed so easy. Just stop! Lee and the kids were real happy about it. Only Lee knew how bad it had been.

I did stop drinking. I was at the UCLA Center a little more than two weeks. While I was there, not drinking, my weight went down. I began to feel better about myself. I *could* stop drinking, because I *had* stopped drinking!

However, the tests they took—not only blood tests, but a liver biopsy—showed that my liver had become enlarged three or four times over. While I was there it shrank back. But even before I left there, I started to blow it back up again.

Since I couldn't have vodka and tonic, I asked the doctor if I could drink a little tonic. That way I could ease off. He said that would be fine. But it didn't taste too good, so I asked Lee to bring me a little bottle of bitters, just to flavor it. He thought that would be all right, so he did. And I asked other visitors to bring me little bottles. The bitters made the tonic taste better. The more bitters, the better the taste. But bitters are fifty percent alcohol. After a while my tonic drink was as dark as bourbon and almost as lethal.

During my stay there, I was fitted for a formal gown and checked out long enough to take part in a fiftieth anniversary birthday party for CBS. My weight was down, so I looked good. I ate and drank. Then I checked back into the hospital.

I had a VIP suite. I could order my meals from outside. Lee often had dinner with me. We were living high on the hog, as if I didn't really have a problem.

When they released me, Lee and I went to the San Diego area for a few days to get away by ourselves. It was around Christmas and it was very nice. I didn't drink, and it looked as though we were doing something about my problem. I didn't even drink on New Year's Eve.

I came back terribly proud of having spent a weekend sober—and my doctor knocked me right off my perch. He announced that I was a liar, that all alcoholics are liars, and that tests showed my liver was diseased from drink. He said I had to face the fact that I was a drunk, and that I had to either stop drinking, get help to stop drinking, or die from drinking, but he doubted that I could stop, because alcoholics can't stop on their own.

I think he thought it best to be blunt with me, but he was, in fact, so cruel that I left his office in tears of rage and went home and started to drink again. I told Lee how terrible the doctor had been to me and was furious with Lee when he wasn't sympathetic. I stewed for a week, drinking steadily, then went to the doctor and told him how terrible I thought he was for having talked to me the way he had. He told Lee he couldn't treat me anymore. I told him I didn't want him to.

I saw I had to have help. I didn't want to die. I was killing myself and I couldn't stop myself. I felt so worthless. I loathed myself. By now, I was drinking to drown my sorrows over my drinking. I wanted to forget what my life was, but the alcohol couldn't kill my thoughts for me—it only confused me. I went to bed and passed out drunk every night.

15

Lee found me another doctor, and this one recommended that I see a psychiatrist. Lee had to plead with me to get me to agree to go. It seemed disgraceful to me, as it does to so many people. But I agreed to go. Then the one the doctor recommended told Lee he couldn't see me because he was carrying too heavy a case load. I thought that let me off the hook. But Lee went to our church to see if one of the people at the counseling center he had helped to set up would recommend a psychiatrist. I should have had counseling at my own church, but I was too embarrassed to tell my troubles to people so close to me. Anyway, Lee got the name of another psychiatrist, who agreed to see me.

Lee went with me the first time. During the first session we accomplished little. I was supposed to tell him my story, but he didn't want to rush me. So we stared at each other for a long time. Eventually he said that he wondered why I had come if I wasn't going to tell him why I had come. I told him I came because my husband wanted me to; that he thought I was an alcoholic, but I thought I was just a heavy drinker, and that my problem wasn't that I drank too much but that my husband thought I drank too much, and *he* was my real problem. Lee loved that. After an hour we left and went home and I got drunk.

The next morning I felt terrible about what I had done, so I called the psychiatrist back and apologized for my behavior and asked him if he would continue to see me. He said he would, so I started to go to him. He asked me about my personal and professional life, and I couldn't tell him anything that I thought caused me to drink too much. Maybe there was something there, but I couldn't see it, and I still can't.

It didn't work the way it does in the movies, where *Ah-ha!* suddenly you realize you do what you do because your dad abused you or your mother was a drunkard or you drowned your puppy, and in that instant you are cured and you never drink again or you stop killing people or something like that.

After a while I was wracking my brains during the drive to his office to think up things to tell him, as if it were a test and I would fail if I couldn't come up with a clue for him. He was a Beverly Hills psychiatrist who charged accordingly.

Well, he treated me, if you want to call it that, but he didn't help me. I didn't hold back anything from him but he didn't have much to say to me, and he didn't help me. Maybe he thought I was holding back things from him. Maybe I bored him. After a while he started stealing glances at his watch. Well, I wanted to get out of his office, too. I wanted to go get a drink.

Before long he and my new doctor agreed I needed extensive treatment and suggested that Cedars Sinai Hospital had a program that would help me. I thought it would be like the UCLA Medical Center, where I would have a private room, be able to order nice meals, and maybe not drink for a week or so.

Lee signed me in the last week of February, 1978. He came with me when a nurse took me to my ward. We passed through a steel door, and when suddenly it slammed shut behind me, I realized I was on one side of the door and Lee was on the other side. There was something about that heavy door and the way it slammed shut behind me and wouldn't budge when I tried the handle that made me know for sure that I was in a psycho ward.

I threw myself at the door. Through the window I could see Lee turn to leave. I screamed at him not to abandon me. I screamed and screamed. I said I'd do anything if he'd just take me home. I begged and begged, but he just kept walking, without looking back. I didn't even know if he could hear me. He told me later he could and that it was the hardest thing he'd ever had to do in his life to just keep walking away from me, but that he had been warned that I would react as I did, and if he wanted me to be helped he'd just have to walk away. I was hysterical; more scared than I had ever been in my life.

They took me to my room. Along the way, I saw some sad cases of obviously troubled people. I sat down on my bed and realized that I too was a sad case of a troubled person. I didn't think I was crazy, but I knew that crazy people never think they're crazy. For the first time, I realized I really was an alcoholic. But all I had to do was stop drinking and I'd stop being an alcoholic.

I wanted desperately to get out of there, but I realized I was stuck. For a while, at least. I figured I had to convince them I would quit drinking if I hoped ever to get out.

At supper that evening, I sat at a table with three other women patients. When one of them said, "What are *you* here for?" I found myself saying, "I'm an alcoholic."

Later, when a doctor came, I asked him if I could call Lee to apologize because he would be worried about me, and the doctor said I could.

I couldn't get Lee at home so I tried Phil's house and found Lee there. I admitted I was an alcoholic now and told him I was sorry I had behaved so badly because I was so scared, but I would do what I was told so I could be cured as soon as possible so he could come to take me home as soon as possible. He said he never wanted to hurt me, but he wanted me to get help, and he still loved me, and not to worry because our life soon would be as beautiful as it had been before.

I fell asleep, lonely, forlorn, and weeping, feeling lost, as if my lovely life had ended, and had nightmares all night.

In the morning I got a grip on myself. I told myself I would make the best of it. I remembered that Emerson had said attitudes were more important than facts. It was something I had read once and never forgotten. In a way, I had lived by it. I figured out that I couldn't change the fact that I was where I was, but if I took the right attitude toward it I would come out of it all right. I had to be helped, and if I welcomed the help I got here I would be helped and it would all be worthwhile and I would get out and be better because I had been here.

All my life I had looked on the bright side of things. I was an "up" person. I decided I was going to look on the bright side of this experience and be as cheerful as I could, whatever happened. I did not know what would take place, but I prepared myself to deal well with it, whatever it was.

It wasn't much. They dried me out and gave me a lot of shots and other medicine which was supposed to calm me down. I think they thought I would get the DT's while I was kicking my habit cold turkey, but I never did. Somehow, when alcohol wasn't available to me, I didn't miss it. It's strange, but I found my experiences did not fit the expected experiences. Maybe I wasn't a classic case. Maybe there is no such thing.

A psychiatrist talked to me a few times, but didn't get too deep into me. One of the things that bothered me was that there didn't seem to be any other alcoholics among the inmates. No one was quite right, but they weren't drinkers, as far as I could tell. Many were kicking drug habits. I didn't get any specialized treatment or counseling, which I supposed I needed. It was as though they thought all they had to do was dry me out and I would be all right after that. Or maybe that was all they could do. I don't want to put the place down too much, because maybe what they do works for some people, but whatever it was, it didn't work for me.

From the moment I was locked in that prison of a psycho ward I saw how easy it would be to go over the deep edge and lose your sense of the way things should be. I don't know that an alcoholic is any better than an insane person. How do you grade those things? I could see where some might drink to lose sight of their problems and others might simply close their minds to their problems. I didn't want to be there, and I could see how easy it might be to shut my mind to being there.

I had different roommates, all strange in one way or another. One of them was a lovely lady who just didn't seem to make much sense. She was very refined and was upset by the language of the other patients. I don't know if she knew who I was or if it would have mattered to her, but I think she felt I shared her sensibilities, and she clung to me as if I were her friend. I was as kind to her as I could be and tried to help her, but I never figured out what her problem was. They moved her in with me because I was the only one who could get her to go to meals or to arts and crafts or whatever, so there I was, nursing my roommate.

107

Lee visited me often and seemed pleased by my progress. I hadn't been drinking, but I was cheerful. I told him I didn't want to drink anymore and hoped to be released soon.

Lee talked to the head doctor about it and he said they wouldn't release me yet because I wasn't ready to be released, but since I had been on my best behavior he would release me for one week if I agreed to start with Alcoholics Anonymous before I went to Arizona, where I was scheduled to do a play. I agreed not to drink while I was gone, and agreed to return as soon as the play was done.

I'd have agreed to anything just to get out of there, even for only a little while.

Lee had spoken to someone at our church whose wife was a member of Alcoholics Anonymous, and he got her to invite me to a meeting of her group. It was held at a little church in the Valley. When we got there, it turned out to be all women. So Lee left, the women sat around a table, and each one talked about the experiences that had led her to drink. It seemed to me each was trying to top the others. The lower you got, the better you looked. Can you top this? They were bragging about year-long love affairs and two-week drinking binges.

When it came my turn, I told them I drank too much; I admitted I was an alcoholic, but I couldn't tell them why. I said my husband was faithful, loving, sympathetic, and supportive, and my children posed no problems. I said my career had been successful and I led a good life. They seemed disappointed, as if I had to be holding out on them. I couldn't understand that if it was easy to pinpoint your problem, *whoosh*, no problem, right? They were sarcastic to me.

After the meeting, the woman I knew from the church, whom I did not know well, a very domineering type of person, grabbed me and said I had to come to meetings until they could break down my resistance, that it takes three months even to get the sauce out of one's system, and that it would take longer for them to get through to me, and I had to be there this time and that time and the time after that. It turned me off completely.

The whole business just didn't turn me on. I didn't see how it could help me. Professionals had problems reaching people, and these certainly weren't professionals. They'd each had a bad drinking experience, but each experience is different. Maybe knowing you're not the only person in the world with a drinking problem is something. Maybe knowing you could call on one of them to take the bottle out of your hand in the middle of the night when you were about to go off the wagon is a lot. But somehow it wasn't enough for me.

I don't want to put AA down, I really don't. Their way works for many, but I didn't get out of it what I wanted.

Lee was disappointed. By then it seemed to him that I really didn't want to be helped, that I would resist anyone who tried to help me. I wondered about this myself. I wasn't sure of myself anymore. When you are as mixed up as I was, you stop seeing things as they are and start to wonder what's real and what isn't.

Lee and I were a little at odds then. He didn't know what he could do with me or for me, and I didn't know what I wanted from him. My freedom, I suppose. Not freedom from my marriage. Not divorce. Just the freedom to go back to being whoever I wanted to be and to do whatever I wanted to do. Drink or not drink, as I wanted, I guess.

But I seemed to be in control of myself, and we agreed it might be good for me to get away by myself for a week. He was too busy to take off for Phoenix with me, and I was going to do something I knew how to do and had done many times before.

But when I got there I had trouble with my lines. I'd done *Cactus Flower* many times before, but I kept forgetting them. I wasn't drinking then, but maybe the damage had already been done. Again, I wondered if my mind was going.

I figured I'd get through it, get back into the groove. I didn't realize how badly I was embarrassing myself. I was surprised when Lee suddenly showed up. He said he'd just changed his mind and wanted to be with me, but I found out later they'd sent for him because they were worried I couldn't do the show and they didn't know what was wrong with me.

They didn't know I was just temporarily out of an institution. If they had, they wouldn't have taken a chance on me. It really wasn't fair to them. But Lee worked with me and I got back into the groove, and I played the piece as though it fit me like an old glove for several nights.

It took all the strength I could get together just to get through the week. When it was done, I felt a letdown. I knew I'd have to go back to the hospital, and I didn't want to. I begged Lee to let me go home for a while. He agreed.

I was home almost two months. But of course I began to drink again. I began to bloat up again. Lee felt I should go back. It was as if the only way I could prove I wanted to stop drinking was to agree to go back. It was as if Lee were my father and I was his daughter who had to do what daddy felt was best for me. I felt helpless and hated it.

So in May, 1978, I returned to Cedars Sinai. Lee signed me back in. The metal door slammed shut behind me. I was back in prison. I crawled into bed and wept. When I awoke the next morning my roommate, the elegant lady, was standing nude by the dresser. She always wanted to eat with me, so I told her to get dressed and we'd go to breakfast, but she just stood there.

I called a nurse, who brought two others in. They forced this lovely lady down on her bed. She fought like an animal as they dressed her. It was awful. They dragged her down the hall and shoved her into the meal line. But the minute they left her, she took off.

When I got back to our room, she was there. She had taken off her clothes and left them on the floor, and she was standing naked by the dresser again. This went on for days. They'd forcibly dress her and drag her somewhere, but when they left her, she would return to the room and undress and take up her position again.

After a while, they said they were sorry but they'd have to lock our room so she couldn't get back in when she wasn't supposed to be there; and if I wanted to go in the room to go to the bathroom or anything, I'd have to get them to open up for me. That was a terrible burden to lay on me, and it made me feel very guilty.

They weren't helping her. Whatever they were doing to her didn't help her. I felt sorry for her, but at the same time it was hard living with her. I wasn't alone, yet I was alone.

Her husband came to see her every visiting hour. He often talked to Lee about her. He told Lee she had simply lost touch with reality and he had no idea why. I think Lee could see that being with her couldn't help me. Also, I was back on medication, and apparently I was beginning to become lethargic, almost a vegetable. Lee decided to take me out of there.

My first stay had been less than two weeks. It seemed like two months. My second stay was a little less than four weeks. It seemed like four months. All told, I spent almost six weeks in that hospital.

Before I could go, I had to meet with the head doctor. Maybe he was annoyed because I was being taken away before he was ready to release me. He asked me if I felt I had been helped. I said I hoped so, but I didn't know what had been done for me except get me away from my bottle. He asked me if I had wanted to be helped, and I swore I had.

He had a clipboard full of reports on me from the nurses and others. As we talked, he was reading through these and making faces. I asked him what they said, because I wanted to know. The reports said I had been putting on a pretty good act for everyone but I wasn't fooling anyone with my cheerful attitude, and it was superficial of me to try.

I couldn't believe it. Because I had been the one person who had tried to make the best of things and be agreeable with others I was "superficial"? I said, "Do you mean to say one of the nurses actually said that about me?" He seemed to take delight in saying, "Not just one; they all said the same thing." I was hurt terribly by it.

I left with the same problem I had when I went in. I hope they were able to help others, but they didn't help me. Maybe others were meant to be there, but I wasn't. They took my problem from me temporarily, but they didn't deal with it.

Maybe they were better with psychiatric problems than with alcoholism.

I was beginning to wonder if there was *anyone* who could help me.

16

The day I was signed out of Cedars Sinai I was signed into Las Encinas. Lee drove me directly from Cedars Sinai in Beverly Hills to Pasadena. I didn't even have time to get a drink.

At Cedars Sinai, alcoholism was treated as a mental illness. I had had counseling sessions there with psychiatrists and psychologists and in group, but the thrust of these was to find out what triggered my drinking. When they couldn't find a cause for my problem, they assumed I was holding out.

At Las Encinas I found a place that was more like a country club than a hospital. There were recreational activities like volleyball, and arts and crafts programs, and I took up painting. There was a beauty shop where I had my hair and nails done regularly.

The first thing they do at all of these places is dry you out. They keep you away from alcohol and give you pills to help get it out of your system. Then they had the same sort of counseling sessions that I'd been through at Cedars in which they sought a clue to your condition. When I told them my life had been beautiful, full of blessings, they were annoyed with me, again as if I were holding out. But there was one psychiatrist I really liked and talked to fairly often. He tried to understand me. I didn't understand myself. I should have been happy. I shouldn't have had to drink. I didn't know why I drank. I couldn't give him a clue. Like the others, he looked for reasons and was mystified.

I Ain't Down Yet

At Las Encinas they allow you weekend leave to go home. I went home every weekend. And drank.

I didn't tell them I was drinking on the weekends, but I'm sure they knew. They put me on antabuse. They explained to me that it would make drinking distasteful to me and if I drank it would make me very sick. I didn't dare refuse. Supposedly, I would accept anything that would cure me of my alcoholism. The first time a nurse came in with an antabuse pill, she gave me the other pills, then the antabuse. I swallowed each with water in turn, then gasped suddenly and said I had to go to the bathroom, taking the antabuse pill with me.

I flushed it down the toilet, then told her I'd taken it.

I did that with nurse after nurse. But I couldn't do it with the same one more than once, so I'd stick the pill under my tongue and only pretend to swallow it. Or palm it in my hand and only pretend to put it in my mouth.

If you've ever tried to teach a child to swallow a pill, you know it is very hard if he's afraid and his throat tightens up. It was easy for me to make my throat so tight the pill wouldn't pass through.

I spat them out in the toilet.

A couple of times, however, smart nurses trapped me. They'd take the pill back before I went to the bathroom, then hand it back to me and watch while I swallowed it. I'd say I didn't want them to have to wait for me, but they'd just laugh.

One time I went home five days after I'd taken an antabuse pill. I got off by myself and got myself a drink of vodka. I couldn't believe that stuff was still in my system. It was. I felt the most awful sensation in my body. I could hardly breathe. I staggered to the bathroom because I thought I was going to throw up. No such luck. I looked in the mirror. My face was flushed bright red.

I called for Lee. I thought I was going to die. He came and calmed me down. By then, the sensation was passing. I didn't tell him what had happened, other than I thought I was having a reaction to the medication I was taking.

But he spoke to the doctors at Las Encinas, who told him what must have happened. He knew I was sneaking drinks while I was home and he was deeply discouraged. So was I.

I suspect only a little bit of the antabuse was still in my system when I took that drink. Thus, the reaction was brief and passed swiftly. But it was so severe it was frightening.

I seldom have felt so horrible. Antabuse isn't a cure for drinking but it scares you away from it. If you want to drink, of course, you simply stop taking the stuff.

At that point, I thought I wanted to be cured, but the need to sneak drinks was too much for me to resist.

I was at Las Encinas a long time. So long that Lee had to tell the kids and our closer friends and those who did business for me the truth. I hated that, but it had to be. However, there were no stories in the newspapers or anything. At that point, I supposed I wasn't that important. Now I know the press simply didn't know, because once I told them, I attracted a lot of attention.

At Las Encinas, I kept to myself, stayed in my room a lot, watched television a lot, read a little. Weekends, I'd go home and drink. The weeks went by and I was just putting in time.

I was lethargic when Lee came to call. I didn't care about anything. If he thought I should continue there, that was all right with me. Whatever he wanted was all right with me. My life as I had known it was over.

It didn't bother me to go without a drink all week. I could drink on the weekends. There was no way Lee could stop me. I had bottles hidden. He searched for them, but never found them all.

I couldn't be locked in my room forever, any more than I could have my mouth taped shut forever. I couldn't be compelled to take antabuse all the time. All he could do was give up on me. I don't know why he didn't.

I had given up on myself.

I don't really know how hard it was on Lee. Later, we talked about it a little, but not a lot. It is difficult to put your emotions into words. And we didn't want to dwell on the past.

I think Lee would lay down his life for me. Nevertheless, I think it is easier to walk away from someone's death bed than it is to be lying there dying. You walk out into the fresh air and sunshine. You have to be happy you're alive, that it's not you dying.

To be honest, I think it was easier for Lee to walk away from me at Cedars Sinai than it was for me to be stuck on the other side of the door. I'm not as strong as he is. He's had low points in his life, but he never hit bottom.

I *had* hit it, the lowest point of my life. I was sitting around in a nice room reading a little, and I might as well have been in the gutter on skid row.

Somehow, I had come to accept my alcoholism. All right, I said to myself, this is the way it is; this is what I have to live with; this is what Lee has to live with; this is what the kids have to live with; this is what anyone who wants to live with me has to live with.

I was at the Las Encinas Hospital for nearly twenty weeks. It was like taking a long vacation from life. I felt as if I'd left my family and friends, resigned from the human race. The worst thing was that I wasted my time; I didn't get anything out of it.

Maybe I didn't want to get anything out of it. I thought I did, though. But I just wasn't helped.

If I hadn't been helped at Raleigh Hills I would have had to admit that I didn't want to be or couldn't be helped. I had been in two places where I was supposed to get help and I had given up hope. I'd spent almost a year going from place to place, seeking help, getting none, unable to help myself. If Lee had given up, I'd still be drinking. I'd be a poor excuse for a person.

Hello. I'm Gale Storm. In the past I have been telling you about my treatment for alcoholism at Raleigh Hills Hospital. With their help, I have become completely indifferent to alcohol. Now, I would like to share my feelings about sobriety with you: Today, because of Raleigh Hills, I feel great—physically, mentally, and spiritually. I like my life today. If you have a drinking problem, and want help, call Raleigh Hills.

Television commercial,
western states, 1980

Thom Schneidt
Administrator

Raleigh Hills Hospital
Oxnard, California

Less than fifty years ago, there was very little specialized treatment available to alcoholics. Sometimes regarded as criminals, they were often incarcerated to prevent them from hurting themselves or harming others.

In 1942, Raleigh Hills Hospital opened its first treatment facility. The treatment program was designed to make alcohol less appealing to the alcoholic.

Today, Raleigh Hills Hospitals, now a branch of Advanced Health Systems, has established alcoholism treatment facilities throughout the western and midwestern United States. The establishment of new programs and new hospitals is continuing. The Raleigh Hills Foundation, created in the 1960s, is a leading alcoholism research organization.

What is an alcoholic, anyway? You have to start there if you are going to provide treatment. There are many different definitions. Some say alcoholics drink more than other people, won't admit it, are irritated by discussions of it, avoid family and friends while drinking to avoid discussions of it, turn to drink after arguments about it, turn to drink during stressful situations, can't "hold their liquor," can't cut down, can't stop, and so on.

We take the position that an alcoholic is someone who feels the *need* to drink and whose drinking is disturbing his or her professional and private life.

A lot of drinkers think they're not alcoholics because they don't drink during the week, they don't drink before five in the evening, they don't get drunk, or they're not on skid row. We estimate that there are more than six million alcoholics in this country; only about 3 percent of them are falling-down drunks. Body chemistry is an individual matter; some people are affected less by drink than others, but alcoholism inevitably inhibits one's powers of reason and judgment and the ability to evaluate oneself or one's actions critically. Many alcoholics continue to function effectively in their families and their jobs for a while, but eventually drink is going to affect them.

We consider alcoholism a disease. Alcoholics are allergic to the chemical ethyl alcohol, which is intoxicating and addicting. It is commonly known to be damaging to the liver, but it is also damaging to the brain—to almost every part of the body, in fact. Alcohol is burned up by the body in the liver, but when it accumulates, the liver loses its efficiency in metabolizing it.

It is not what you drink or when you drink, but whether you can tolerate what you drink that matters. Many can stop for prolonged periods. It is not whether you can stop drinking that matters, but whether you start again. Alcohol is a drug. One of the oldest drugs known to man, it is as addictive and dangerous to the alcoholic as heroin or any other narcotic would be to the addict of those drugs.

Raleigh Hills Hospitals are exclusively designed to treat the alcoholic man or woman. Many who come to us are also dependent on soft drugs, frequently prescribed for them because of some physical or psychological damage drink may have done to them. Many are suffering from illnesses related to their drinking. Thus we have to also function to some degree as a standard hospital, certified nationally as well as by the states we are in. But we accept only those patients who have a primary alcoholic abuse problem. Beyond that we do not discriminate in any way as to whom we accept.

I served as a counselor here at the Oxnard hospital, north of the San Fernando Valley, before becoming the administrator. This is the facility to which Gale Storm came and continues to come, since we have a program of continuing treatment and reinforcement and welcome the return of former patients so long as they remain sober.

The treatment period is brief but intense, depending for length (usually two weeks) on the degree of the patient's problem. In many cases, treatment is covered by medical insurance. If a patient has financial difficulties, we try to work out long-range programs of payment.

We make use of every minute in our short program. Each hospital takes care of no more than thirty-five to fifty patients at a time, and each patient receives concentrated individual attention. We do not have television sets, reading rooms, or recreational

In a romantic mood with Dan Duryea in Al Jennings of Oklahoma, *1951.*

The Honey Harris Collection

As a movie star, not only could I drive fancy cars; I was also permitted to pump my own gas.

Christmas, 1951.

Either Lee is kissing me goodbye as he leaves for work or the milkman is kissing me hello!

CBS photo by Walt Davis

They just loved to use animals on "Margie." One of my favorites was this boxing kangaroo Don Hayden is bringing in for a visit.

In a particularly explosive "Margie" episode, Clarence Kolb's cigar has blown up all over Charlie Farrell and me. Clarence played Mr. Honeywell. I played the bearded Scot.

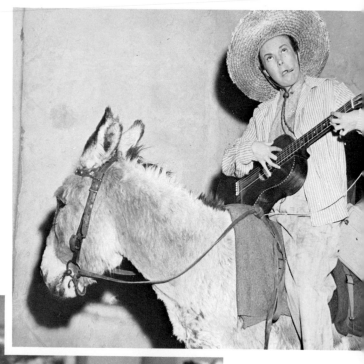

A Gay Caballero astride my mighty steed during one "Margie" episode.

Margie meets her match when she finds fault with the glue the postal service uses on stamps.

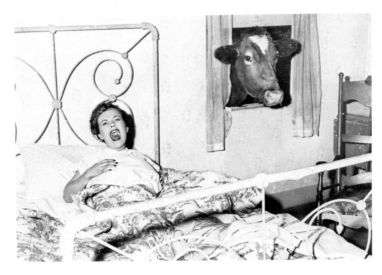

Above: *Margie graciously greets a guest.*

Below: A *"boom-boom-boom" production number in the first episode of "The Gale Storm Show: Oh! Susanna,"* 1956. Who'd ever guess this dancer was an expectant mother again?

Above: *Clearly, I am concerned with the shenanigans in the script for my television series, "My Little Margie," which began in 1952.*

The happy homemaker with sons, at home.

Above: ZaSu Pitts and I display our Hollywood glamour and poise in "Oh! Susanna."

Little old me and Gertrude Hoffman ("Mrs. Odetts") in an episode from "Margie."

Below: Caught in the act as I am about to don a costume with my dear costar, ZaSu Pitts, in "Susanna."

Above: During a ten-week Texas tour of Plaza Suite with Tyler McVey in the 1970s, I played three different roles. This one featured a distressed knee.

Photos by Sylvia Cary

Wearing the uniform of the day—pajamas and robe—I, as a graduate, encourage patients at Raleigh Hills Hospital in Oxnard, California.

facilities. We prefer to have patients concentrate on their problems and how to solve them. If they read, they read literature on alcoholism. They receive one-to-one counseling, participate in group therapy, and listen to lectures. They come to understand themselves and their problems as they never have before. They are shown the way to overcome obstacles that may once have seemed insurmountable.

I don't want it to sound easy. It isn't. We are just coming to see how complicated the disease is, how difficult it is for those afflicted with it to deal with it. We attack it from every angle, in the hope that one way or another we will reach everyone where he or she hurts. We are as complete as we can be. Our follow-up program is as important as our primary program. Patients are always welcome to return, and there is never any additional charge. In essence we offer a lifelong system of support.

In our view, an alcoholic is an alcoholic is an alcoholic. He or she cannot be cured of the disease, but he can learn to live with it. They are shown that while they cannot tolerate drink, they can *avoid* drink, and so live normal lives, just as diabetics cannot tolerate sugars, but can avoid them and so live normal lives. We bring their families into the program so they can understand the problem and provide support, too.

We provide simple but comfortable surroundings. Doors are not locked. Patients are free to leave at any time. We recognize that they may have been abused by others, that they may be suffering remorse and depression. So we try to provide a haven for them, with warmth and welcome. Many members of our staff are former patients who understand what patients are going through and provide excellent examples of recovery for them.

Our patients come from every walk of life; they may be wealthy or poor, successful or not. The disease does not discriminate.

More men than women come to us, but we assume this is only because in this society it is easier for women to hide their alcoholism. Women have been coming to us in greater numbers, however, since Gale Storm began doing commercials for us. Our ratio is currently 40 percent women.

Through forty years of experience, we have developed a specific system of treatment. We begin with a complete physical examination. Then we ask patients to undergo psychological evaluation, so we can understand them and their particular problems as fully as possible. We want to work with them while they are here so that when they return to their social and professional lives as non-drinkers they will be able to assert themselves and function effectively. We also have programs that counsel families and employers. Eventually they too come to see that alcoholism is a disease that can be tolerated and overcome.

Patients are detoxified in the most comfortable and humane manner possible, using a procedure that minimizes the consequences of withdrawal. This usually consists of administering small doses of alcohol at regular intervals, decreasing the dosage steadily over a two- to five-day period—a time span dictated by the degree of the alcoholic's state of intoxication. This slow withdrawal method reduces the likelihood of such severe medical problems as delirium tremens and seizures.

After detoxification the patient is ready for treatment. Raleigh Hills's therapeutic approach is comprised of five steps: conditioning procedures, physical rehabilitation, social rehabilitation, formal psychotherapy, and specialized procedures.

Conditioned reflex treatments take place on five alternating days. An injection of medication is given by a specially trained treatment technician (under the direction of a physician) to produce nausea and discomfort. Then the patient is given a variety of alcoholic beverages with instructions to "smell, swish and swallow." The added nausea that this causes becomes associated with the smell, sight and taste of alcohol. Instead of eliciting a pleasurable response, alcohol becomes distasteful.

The treatment isn't pleasant, but it is effective. Have you ever eaten some particular food that was sour or bad in some way? Have you noticed how you no longer wanted to eat that food, in fact felt sick at the thought of it? We apply this behavioral conditioning to alcoholics. They are made to experience drink in so distasteful a way that they will thereafter turn away from the taste and smell of alcohol by reflex.

Conditioned reflex treatments are combined with counseling sessions, biofeedback instruction, aftercare consultation, anxiety management training, round-table discussions, as well as individual and group psychological sessions. After completing two weeks of intensive conditioning and counseling treatments, the chances of the patient's (referred to now as a recovering alcoholic) remaining sober and recuperating from the effects of alcohol addiction are excellent.

To aid in this commitment, six follow-up treatments (called recaps) are scheduled over the next twelve months. These booster sessions reinforce the conditioning process, making it easier for the recovering alcoholic to remain sober.

The treatment team works with each individual to develop a specific treatment plan comprised of a tightly structured schedule of activities designed to assist the patient to deal effectively with his or her alcoholism throughout each day in the program. Patients are encouraged to approach staff members any time they are troubled. They are given a bill of patients' rights on entering so they know they can ask anything about any treatment any time they wish, so they know they are not prisoners and are free to proceed with the program or drop out of it at any time they wish.

During the hospital stay patients are helped to formulate a reasonable set of goals and objectives. We encourage them to join Alcoholics Anonymous, and family members are encouraged to participate in Al-Anon meetings.

Any time a former Raleigh Hills patient feels that his sobriety is in jeopardy, he may return to any Raleigh Hills facility for an additional recap treatment or counseling session. So long as the recovering alcoholic remains sober, Raleigh Hills will do everything possible to help him stay that way.

Gale Storm takes advantage of this because she feels comfortable here and she can give comfort and help to others here. She volunteered to do commercials for us because she wants others to be helped as she was.

It took considerable courage for a performer as popular as she has been to admit publicly that she was an alcoholic. She did it because she feels she can reach more alcoholics than many others possibly can.

The problem of alcoholism in this country goes far beyond what most people realize. If there are 100 million drinkers in this country, one out of ten probably is an alcoholic. Perhaps 60 percent of the divorces in this country can be related to some amount of alcoholism.

Probably 50 percent of the job firings in this country can be related to alcoholism. Some 50 percent of the car accidents on our roads involve alcohol; half of those involve alcoholics. Forty percent of the admissions to mental hospitals involve alcoholics. Forty percent of the murders in this country are believed to be committed by alcoholics.

We have to try to help these people. At Raleigh Hills Hospitals we think we succeed.

17

I might have given up on getting help, but Lee would not let me. Through one of his business associates he heard about Raleigh Hills and wanted me to try it. He kept talking about it and talking about it.

"Right after New Year's," I kept saying, putting it off as if it would never come. I tried not to drink when Lee was looking. Just a little, so he'd think I could handle it. I kept trying to tell myself I *could* handle it—that maybe I was the exception to the rule.

I got through the holidays at the end of 1978, but I could see that the kids were concerned. I had put on weight again, so I supposed my liver was swelling up again, but I kept telling myself I was just eating too much. A lot of my Christmas presents were new clothes in larger sizes. My New Year's resolution was to swear off the bottle forever. I finished one bottle and got another one on New Year's Day.

What I didn't know at the time, and didn't learn until much later, was that Lee was then going to Al-Anon meetings. I knew he'd gone to *one:* he'd told me after supper one evening that he was on his way to try the AA "auxiliary." When he came home he found me, vodka in hand, staring at the television set.

"Honey," he told me, his voice almost disbelieving, "they told me I'm sicker than you are!"

"Good," I remember snapping, "now maybe we can get somewhere."

After several meetings, Lee had absorbed one of Al-Anon's most important tenets: as the partner of an alcoholic, you must learn to "let go" of him or her. It is pointless to cajole or wheedle or try to force an alcoholic to do something for his or her own good. Lee took the lesson to heart, and simply stopped trying to direct my recovery.

Finally—and maybe because Lee *wasn't* pressing me—I gave up and gave in. I asked Lee to take me to Raleigh Hills. So on the 22nd of January, 1979, he drove me to Oxnard, about an hour north of us, near the ocean. It didn't look like a hospital. It was a plain one-story building just off a busy street. My room was plain, without television or radio. There were two beds. I didn't want to be with anyone else. I wasn't, as it turned out, because they weren't overcrowded. I think they had fourteen rooms, enough for twenty-eight patients, but had only seventeen at the time.

Lee signed me in. I was surprised to find that my stay there would be only two to three weeks. That didn't sound too bad. I could do that standing on my head by then. I was told I had to abide by the rules as long as I was there, but I could leave anytime I wanted. So I wasn't a prisoner, although I knew Lee wouldn't want me to leave. After a while you go into one of those places wondering how soon you can get out. After a while you don't really think about being helped.

Lee kissed me goodbye and told me he loved me.

They gave me a manual to read which explained that I would be told in detail about every stage of my treatment and I could ask questions about anything I didn't understand. This was all contained in what the hospital called "A Patient's Bill of Rights."

I was given a pair of men's pajamas, a pair of slippers, and a robe. They would keep me provided with clean clothes, but these were what I was to wear. My regular clothes—and I had a suitcase full—were taken from me. This was so that all patients would be equal as they moved around the area. No one would be better dressed than anyone else. No one was better than anyone else, whatever they were in the outside world. I was vain enough to want to be recognized. But I got used to this, too. Everyone was on a first-name basis. I was Gale, and no one asked me about television, movies, or anything like that. If I acted as if I didn't want to talk, we didn't talk. Everyone was so nice that gradually I started to talk. The doctors, nurses, technicians, and other attendants were all warm and made me feel welcome. Soon I felt at home.

Even before Lee left, they asked me what alcoholic beverage I preferred. I said vodka, and to my surprise they brought me a shot of it. Lee must have been prepared for this, because he didn't seem very surprised. Making light of a tense situation, I sipped it slowly and said, "Hey, this isn't bad. I think I'm going to like it here." They explained that they would detox me gradually so I wouldn't have any severe withdrawal symptoms. In fact, I got a big shot glass of vodka every two hours for the first day I was there.

Gradually, over five days, with careful monitoring, I was completely detoxed. It was like having a comfort blanket very slowly removed, rather than simply yanked away from me.

Following withdrawal and after tests, a doctor came to me with the results. He said, "I'm not going to pull any punches. You have to know your situation. It is serious. Your liver is enlarged and diseased. Your blood has been cleansed of alcohol for the time being and your liver will shrink as long as you stay away from alcohol, but it will swell back up as soon as you return to alcohol, which we hope you will not do. But much of the damage that has been done cannot be undone. And you have no doubt done damage to other parts of your body, including your brain. Alcoholism is a progressive disease. If you do start to drink again, you will begin to do further damage to your body from the point at which you stopped. Before long you will start to have serious physical problems. Eventually you will die."

I want to tell you that man scared me. He wanted to. But he was telling me the truth, whether I wanted to hear it or not. Later, I heard lectures and saw slides and films depicting in the most graphic, frightening way the damage done to the body by alcohol. But I could see for myself it was the truth. It was hard to hear and look at those things, but it had an enormous impact. Alcohol causes a series of chemical reactions within the body which damage and destroy cells until the body and the brain no longer function effectively and, eventually, no longer function at all.

In the early counseling sessions and round-table sessions with other patients and with a doctor or psychologist or nurse, they hammered away at this again and again. It didn't matter that we didn't want to hear it; we had to listen to it. And look at photographs of the organs of people who had died from drink. I pictured myself in those photos. It wasn't a pretty sight.

125

When it came time to start the aversion therapy, I was ready. This was supposed to be the secret to the success of the system. Everyone talked about how bad it was, but how bad could it be? The doctor told me it would be unpleasant, but it wouldn't hurt or anything like that. He also told me I would be a "swisher" instead of a "swallower." He didn't feel I had to swallow the alcohol I would drink during the therapy, but would get the same experience from sniffing each drink, holding each drink in my mouth, swishing it around, then spitting it out. Depending on their degree of health, patients were classified as "swishers" or "swallowers." Most were "swallowers."

Patients take up to five of these aversion therapy treatments over ten days—one every other day. I looked forward to my first treatment because it was supposed to be something that really helped dampen your desire to drink, but I was apprehensive because of the way other patients complained about them and because I could see some patients moaning and groaning in their beds afterwards.

Finally, it was my turn, and I was taken to a room they had been careful to show me beforehand. It was small, and the walls were lined with shelves full of bottles of every kind of alcohol imaginable. In the center of the room was a large barber's chair covered with flannel sheets. Attached to it was a tray with a rinse basin on it. In front of it was a full-length mirror. To one side was a small bathroom. There also was an oxygen tank and an emergency suction machine.

I was wrapped in a wool blanket and given a towel. A nurse gave me a shot of emetine which I had been told induced nausea. Then I was seated in the chair, with a treatment nurse at my side. Near her, set up on a "bar," were glasses of vodka, different kinds of whiskey, and beer that had been allowed to go warm and flat overnight.

I was told to take each one in turn, smell it, swish it in my mouth a fairly long time, then spit it out into the basin. I took each drink in turn and did as I was told. My mouth felt as if it had literally been cauterized—by the stuff I'd been sending through my entire body for years! But I wasn't nauseated at all; after a half-hour I was finished and was taken back to my room.

I was furious. Here I'd waited so long for this treatment, and nothing! After such a big buildup, it was a big letdown. I felt they'd taken it easy on me, after all. I could have killed that doctor, and I sent for him in a rage. When he came, I complained that I was paying my money like anyone else and I had every right to get the full treatment. He assured me I had, and that it was not unusual for a patient to get through the first treatment without a reaction.

I didn't believe him. I wondered if maybe I hadn't gotten a strong enough shot. Or if maybe I should have swallowed the stuff. He assured me that swishing was enough and that I'd probably get a good reaction the next time.

Through the next day and into the following day, when it was time again for me to take a treatment, I was extremely impatient. You've never seen anyone so anxious to get sick.

I got my shot, assured it was a strong one. I sat down and faced another set of six drinks. The first was vodka, my favorite, and I wanted to swallow it, but was warned not to. Then bourbon. Then gin. Then wine. Swishing and spitting. No nausea. I complained it wasn't working. The nurse said not to worry.

Last was the beer. Well, I could certainly swallow that. I was warned not to. So I swished it. All of a sudden the most awful nausea swept over me, and I couldn't control myself as I started to throw up and throw up. As you know, vomiting makes you feel as if your insides are twisting apart. After a minute or so I was through. I looked at myself in the mirror and I was awful.

I felt too terrible to feel satisfied. I was taken back to my room, given a gin-soaked washcloth, and told to lie down and stay there for four hours. I was to sniff the washcloth from time to time. A tray with a basin was pushed by my bed and I was told to throw up into that if I had to. I was definitely not to shower.

I lay there in waves of nausea, not exactly looking forward to the next treatment. The four hours seemed like four days.

But I began to feel better when they brought me some broth and crackers. After I was up and had washed, I went out to the others to tell them my tale of woe, joining the moaners and groaners society.

As they wheeled trays of drinks around to the rooms of patients they were detoxing, I found that if I got a whiff of one I felt nauseated all over again. This time I welcomed my "day off."

At the next treatment I had, as I recall, eight drinks. I don't know whether they also were increasing the strength of the shots, but the first drink, my beloved vodka, made me sick, and when I spat it out I started to throw up. I still had to go on to the second drink. And the third.

The nurses were very nice. Most were former patients, and they told me how they'd gone through this, what a relief it was not to want to drink, how wonderful sobriety was. They kept using that term sobriety.

I got through my eight drinks, sick and gagging all the while. When I saw myself later in the mirror, I was not a glamorous screen star, but some scuzzy excuse for a human being.

I think that by far the most important thing they did for me at Raleigh Hills Hospital was to make me see that alcoholism is a disease. Before that I thought it was a weakness, that it was a condition of my character that I had to drink for whatever reason, that I could not stop no matter how much I wanted to. I thought there had to be a reason why I drank and risked losing my love and my life even if I could not come up with a clue. I suspected I was sick mentally. That, in essence, was what I had been told elsewhere.

It was, Raleigh Hills said, an incurable disease, but it was also one that could be controlled, like diabetes. I could not tolerate alcohol in my system any more than a diabetic can tolerate excess sugar.

It was a great relief to me finally to become convinced that my alcoholism was a sickness I could no more be blamed for than a diabetic can be blamed for his condition. Some people may be driven to drink by problems or failure or unhappiness or whatever, but only those who are allergic to alcohol will become alcoholics. No one really needs a reason to drink to become an alcoholic. Whether or not I had some hidden reason, I craved alcohol. And could not tolerate it. After Raleigh Hills, it was as though a large weight had been lifted off my back. I saw that I was not necessarily psychologically mixed up, but rather that I had a physical problem and should be psychologically able to deal with it. The aversion therapy was devised to deal with the physical problem, but the many and varied counseling sessions were enormously effective in teaching me to understand and handle my problem.

Each week we were given mimeographed sheets spelling out our schedules for that week, hour by hour. I have one in front of me now.

On Monday I had to get up for a 7 A.M. breakfast. At 8 I was to be ready to receive the doctor on his rounds. From 9 to noon I was to have individual counseling and biofeedback training in which I was told what alcohol was doing to me biologically.

From noon to 1, lunch. At 1, a nurse's round-table in which we discussed our disease in its various aspects. At 2, there was a program on family life for the alcoholic. At 3, a film on alcoholism. At 4, an Alcoholics Anonymous orientation lecture. Dinner was at 5. After 6, visitors were permitted.

There were many differences from day to day. There were nurses' round-table sessions, doctors' round-table sessions and psychologists' round-table sessions. There were lectures and films on the medical and psychological aspects of alcoholism and on the values of good nutrition.

There were lectures on learning to relax, on learning to assert ourselves, on developing our self-esteem to the fullest, on developing our personalities to the fullest, on developing our family life to the fullest, on reestablishing our place in life, on setting short-term and long-range goals, and on dealing with success and failure.

All of this may sound simplistic, pretentious and vague, but it was complex, down to earth, and detailed. All of it came from people who had been where we had been, and from experience they spoke a language we understood. All of it dealt with problems we would face and provided practical advice of the sort we could put into effect.

Without the counseling I received at Raleigh Hills I do not know if I could have recovered my sense of self-esteem, of being a worthwhile person, of being important to other people, of having good things to give to other people. I had been negative about myself and my life long enough to have lost all the confidence I had built up through all those years of easy success, and I had to regain my confidence and readopt a positive attitude toward myself and my life.

We were shown that we had to rehabilitate ourselves so we could reenter society. Most of us had surrendered our rights to others who ran us and our families while we devoted ourselves to drink. We had to reclaim our rights and become independent individuals who had a say in how we led our lives. Our families simply would have to be made to see that we no longer were dependent on them and no longer needed them as crutches to get through life.

Many of those who were there had empty lives. I was one of the lucky ones. I would return to a loving family, a nice home, a career that was far from finished.

Lee and I decided, during the few visiting periods, that we wanted to sell our house in Encino. While we'd had wonderful times there, we no longer needed such a large place, so costly to keep up. We wanted to buy a smaller house. And perhaps a vacation place near the ocean.

I wanted to develop my independence enough to be Lee's equal. I wanted to share life with him. I wanted to lose more weight, seek acting assignments, and schedule classical singing lessons, but I also wanted to take a more active part in his insurance business—entertaining his business associates for the first time. And I wanted to take what I had been taught and pass it on to others so perhaps they could be helped as I had been helped. Before I left, I felt stronger than I had in years, sure for the first time that I did not want to drink, did not have to drink, could do without drink.

Once you have stopped killing yourself with drink, you have to figure out how best to start living again.

At Raleigh Hills they treated the whole person and the entire problem. I know that what they do worked for me and has worked for many others.

I'm sorry if this sounds like a commercial, but it explains why I started to do commercials for them. This was my experience with them, and it is a basic part of my story. They are the reason I recovered from my sickness. The staff there could not have been more caring, kinder, or wiser than it was. Everyone who worked with me showed a warmth close to love for me. There were nights when nurses held me in their arms and rocked me while I wept like a child. And there were times when we laughed together at this nonsense we call life.

I came to know well many of the patients there. We discussed our different problems and common experiences with an intimacy that I would have believed impossible before. It was not important who we were or where we came from, only where we were and where we were going. Men and women alike, young and old alike, we were as one, trying to win a very tough battle, trying to climb out of a very deep pit; and we supported one another sympathetically. When we left we went our separate ways, but we formed friendships I will never forget.

As this is put on paper, it is nearly three years since I last had a drink. I have no desire for a drink, and I know I will never drink again. I went into that place on the 22nd of January, 1979, and was discharged on the 6th of February, so I was there only a little more than two weeks, but in that brief time I received an enormous education, and intense training that turned my life around. There were also regularly scheduled return visits, including six additional aversion treatments, and many unscheduled visits, all of which have helped.

Raleigh Hills is cautious. They prefer that we refer to ourselves as "recovering alcoholics." I prefer to call myself a "recovered alcoholic." Thad Eckman, my psychologist there—a wonderful man whom I'll always treasure—said that was all right as long as I was comfortable with it. I know that what I have is incurable, but I also know I am in control of it.

When Lee drove me home from Raleigh Hills Hospital, he asked me hesitantly whether he should leave bottles of alcohol out, hide them, or throw them away. I was glad that he could be so direct about so touchy a subject. I thought it over and decided he should throw them away.

18

When Raleigh Hills released me, the doctors cautioned me that my condition was chronic; the other patients all wished me well.

In the summer of 1979 I was signed to guest-star on an episode of *The Love Boat*. That was cause for celebration, and I asked Lee if we should break out the champagne. He laughed and said he thought not. It wasn't clear whether I would be needed on the first day of shooting. I waited around the house most of the day for a telephone call that might come, while Susie stewed because she wanted me to go somewhere with her. Then at 4 in the afternoon they called. I thought they must be shooting nights. I drove to the studio, went into makeup, then waited. At 7 they closed the set without calling on me. I thought to myself this would be a good excuse to have a drink. But I laughed at myself and didn't have one. They told me they needed me the next day. It turned out I was in every scene they shot. I did well, but it was a long day. Driving home I thought, in the past I'd have thought boy, if anyone deserves a drink, it's me. This time, though, there was no question, no excuse necessary. I not only didn't deserve a drink—I didn't want one.

The fact is, however, I still drink. Diet Dr. Pepper. I have it delivered by the case. I have it delivered to me wherever I am. I am never without it, even in my car or on a plane. It goes where I do. Good old Dr. P. has taken the place of the villain vodka. It gives me something to hold in my hands at parties. Something to drink when I am thirsty, and I am always thirsty.

An alcoholic can find all kinds of excuses for drinking—I'm happy, I'm sad, I'm mad, I'm glad, I'm tired, I'm frightened, I deserve a break, I don't deserve a break, I can't help myself, and so on and so forth. You have to go through all those stages before you realize you can get through them without turning to the bottle.

The only doubts I ever had were misgivings on the drive home from Raleigh Hills: how would it be back in my normal environment? But those doubts evaporated the moment we hit the outskirts of Encino—and they've never returned.

Time passed—a week, two weeks, a month, two months, six months, a year—and I regained the confidence that I could live without drinking, and every day that went by reinforced me in that confidence. It might make a more dramatic story if I told you of times when I held the bottle in my hand or poured myself a drink, then poured it down the sink; but I never really had any desire for one after I left Raleigh Hills.

I carried with me a copy of what Raleigh Hills calls "The Ten Demandments" for recovering alcoholics, which reminded me, among other things, that alcoholism was an illness, not a weakness; that I should take pride in having overcome it; that I dare not take a drink, but I should dare to live.

I was also given a copy of my bill of "Basic Human Rights," which said, among other things, that I had the right to do what I wanted to do and to make my own mistakes; the right to be independent and competitive; the right to refuse a request and to express anger; the right to be treated as an adult and not patronized.

I was as gracious as I could be about it, but I refused a lot of sympathy. I told Lee to stop telling me how wonderful I was every day, as if, if I weren't reassured regularly, I'd fall off the wagon. Lee got back a different wife from the one he sent away. The first time he said we were going to do this or that, you should have seen his face when I said we were going to do no such thing. I was told that sometimes the families of alcoholics subconsciously want to keep them drinking because it keeps them subservient. It wasn't true of Lee, but it took time for him to realize he was no longer the boss who ran our lives, but had to share leadership.

We had arguments about this and that, and when I got angry at him, he was surprised at me. We had always had arguments, though I'm sure no more than other couples, but for a while I had abdicated my right to express my opinions forcefully, and now I had to get it back. I don't think I did it deliberately, but at first there may have been more arguments than usual because I was asserting myself more than I had done in years. I wanted to be an equal partner in our marriage, but it was a while before Lee could welcome me back into that role. Eventually he did, of course, because we always could communicate with each other and were never afraid to tell each other what was on our minds.

There came a time when he did begin to respect my judgment once again, as he had before. One time he made a deal to hire a fellow at his agency, offering to finance him. When he got home and put the terms on paper he realized he could only lose. He told me about it and wondered what he should do. I said he should tell the fellow he'd made a bad deal and was sorry but it would have to be refigured or dropped. He said, "But, gee, honey, I gave my word." I said, "If you are fair with him, perhaps he will be fair with you. Explain to him that you made an honest mistake and would like to work out a new deal that would benefit both of you." He had to be encouraged to call the man, but he did, and the fellow was very nice about it and agreed to rework their agreement. It was not the biggest deal in the world, but it was a big deal to me because I felt I could once again contribute something helpful to my husband. It was wonderful to be welcomed back to that role in our relationship.

For a time, my daughter treated me as though I were on trial; I knew I had to prove myself. I don't think my drinking ever really affected her life a lot, but I suppose I did give up being a mother for a while, and as she grew up she grew away from me. When I tried to reassume my motherly role, she resented it. She'd do things without asking me. If I asked her about something, she'd give me a smart-aleck answer.

I took it for as long as I could. Then one day, after one such scene, I went to her and said, "Susie, you may not want to hear what I have to say, but I have to say it. I don't know if you think my brain has been addled by alcohol or what, but I am your mother, and I am entitled to a little respect. You are old enough to take control of your own life, but if I ask you about something it is only because I care about you, and I do not deserve to be treated like an idiot. I don't know if you know what you've been doing, but I rate more than smart-aleck responses to my questions. I wish you would think about that."

I left then, and finally she came to me to say she was sorry, that she *did* understand, and that she would behave better in the future.

I remembered back to a time when, years before, I had tried to figure out why Susie seemed especially cold and distant. Finally I had asked Lee, "Honey, this is beginning to get to me; am I doing something wrong?" He said he thought he knew what it was. But he wouldn't tell me what it was. Which was maddening. But he said it was important that I figure it out for myself.

I thought and thought. I covered my many shortcomings. I found out I had more faults than a dog has fleas. Everything from being a bad housekeeper to making too many wisecracks. I thought maybe it was because I couldn't teach her things like sewing. If I can't pin it or glue it together, I don't wear it. I even mentioned my drinking. But it wasn't that bad at that time. Lee said he didn't think it was any of those things. Finally, I asked, "It couldn't be my smoking?" He said, "It just might be."

Lee smoked, but I didn't start until the 1950s, after the first three kids were born. It looked sort of sophisticated to me. So I bought some cigarettes and started practicing. I'd watch how others did it and go into the bathroom to try it out. One time Lee went into the bathroom and smelled the smoke and came out asking who'd been smoking in there. I think he thought a man had been visiting, so I confessed. He wasn't for it, but since he smoked himself, he couldn't take too strong a stand against it.

I got to where I smoked about a pack a day, and I really liked it. But this was about when the Surgeon General's report that smoking could kill had come out and everybody was making a big deal about it. Lee said the family noticed that every time an anti-smoking commercial came on television, I went to the kitchen or the bathroom or something. Lee thought my smoking really bothered both Susie and Paul.

One night at dinner I announced I was going to give up smoking. If I had any doubt that this was what was bothering Susie, I didn't after I made my announcement. Tears welled up in her eyes and she started to cry. She came over to me and hugged me and asked me if I really meant it. I said I did, though I have to admit I didn't know if I could. Paul and Lee also seemed thrilled. Which proved they really cared about me, more maybe than I cared about myself.

I did stop. Cold turkey. From that night on, I have not had another cigarette. I guess I wasn't as addicted to smoking as I was to drinking. I enjoyed it while I did it, but I didn't suffer when I stopped. I have never missed it, even when others smoke around me. Lee stopped, too. Which was supportive of him. Something he would do. Just as he stopped drinking.

Looking back on it, it makes me more sure than ever that drinking is a disease. Smoking is an addiction I was able to stop by myself. It can kill, too, so I was the better for giving it up.

After my return from Raleigh Hills, I felt terrific. I was still too plump when I did "The Love Boat," but I lost weight steadily until I got back almost to my former figure. After a while it became easy to make light of my misery. I was allowed to trip over something without being afraid that someone would think I was drunk.

I went back to the hospital religiously on schedule. I had all six of my recaps—returns to the aversion therapy room and the barber chair. I didn't think I needed them, but the hospital did, so that was that. Each was an overnight visit, the first in two weeks after I'd been discharged, the second four weeks after that, the third six weeks after that, and so forth, spacing out until I was through.

I still keep going back. At first maybe I needed to. Not because I thought I was going to drink, but because it was a refuge for me. During the early weeks of my sobriety there were times when I was scared or tense or uncertain about how I was doing, and I knew I could go there and get comfort and be made to feel I was surrounded by strength. I think we all feel sad at times, as if life is crowding in on us, and it is nice if we have a safe place to go. The hospital, with all the alcoholics and all the people treating alcoholics, had become my safe place. I have never trusted psychiatrists, but I trusted Thad Eckman, my psychologist there, and I always talk with him when I go back, so he continues to counsel me in a way. Our talks aren't too heavy, but I bounce things off him and get back a lot of wisdom.

I am not the only graduate who returns regularly. We all find we can help those who are there as sort of volunteer counselors. I have done commercials for Raleigh Hills and have been told a lot of people come for treatment because of me. They feel that if My Little Margie can beat it, so can they.

Lee and I sold our large house and bought a smaller one in the quiet suburban neighborhood of Tarzana, which was built by Edgar Rice Burroughs, who wrote the original Tarzan stories. It is substantial, a nice house, and we are happy with it. We also bought a beach house on Monarch Bay, in Laguna, where we spend a lot of our summertimes and where we will spend a lot of our retirements, if we ever get around to them. Many a Friday afternoon I take off for Oxnard while Lee leaves for Laguna. They save a room for me at Raleigh Hills, while Lee putters around the bay. It gives us a little quiet time, a little space apart. We are reunited Sunday mornings when we go to church, but in some ways Raleigh Hills has become my church.

19

I wanted to share the wonder of Raleigh Hills with other alcoholics, so I offered to do television commercials for the hospital. They were starting to advertise, and I thought if I admitted they had helped me with my alcoholism, others would want to go there to be helped. To my surprise they weren't sure whether to take me up on my offer. I told them I didn't want any pay to do it, though it turned out that as a member of AFTRA, the union, I had to be paid a minimum.

It wasn't that. They were hesitant to tell me what their objection was, but it turned out that their concern was that if I went public and then relapsed, it could be devastating for me.

But after thinking it over, Herb Pratt, the president, and Jack Fahey, the publicity director at Advanced Health Systems, decided to do it.

I was no longer concerned about what people would think. The people at Advanced Health Systems worried about it because it is important to their program to protect the privacy of their patients, but this was my choice, and Lee supported me in it.

The idea Jack Fahey came up with was simply that I would talk directly to the camera, telling the world that I was an alcoholic, that Raleigh Hills Hospitals had helped me with my problem, and that if you had a similar one perhaps they could help you. I wrote out a rough draft, and then Jack and I worked out the exact wording. The

138

commercial was taped in a studio and went on the air on local Los Angeles stations early in 1980.

The reaction was unbelievable. Everyone who came to me or wrote me congratulated me on my courage. Lee and the kids received positive responses and took pride in my stand. It took courage, but not that much. I was telling people I was cured.

There have not been many public personalities who have admitted alcoholism. Betty Ford is one. Joan Kennedy is another. There have not been many performers who have. Dick Van Dyke is one. Dana Andrews is another. And Jan Clayton, the actress who was the mother on the "Lassie" series. I think when people in the spotlight go public with the admission of such a problem, it encourages others to step out of the shadows and do something about it.

I began to get a great deal of mail from people who said if I could do it, they could, too. I began to meet a great many people who said if I could do it, they could. I met many of them at Raleigh Hills. As many men as women, though women seemed to respond especially well. Most of their stories were extremely touching. Fine lives ruined by alcohol. Fine lives restored by treatment.

The first commercial had so much impact that they ran it on stations in communities throughout the West, wherever Raleigh Hills had a hospital. They put it on network television. They put it on prime time. They asked me to do a second. Then a third. And a fourth. By now, I have done five and look forward to more. You may not see them in the East, but they are all over the West, wherever they have hospitals, all the time.

Raleigh Hills's business has doubled—they have twice as many hospitals now as they did before my first commercial. They asked me to travel to participate in the opening of each new hospital. They asked me to visit their established hospitals. They asked me to speak at ceremonies like anniversaries at all their facilities, new and old alike. They asked me to give magazine, newspaper, radio, and television interviews about my experiences with their hospital. The demand for interviews has been unbelievable. Wherever I go I am asked for them. Phone requests come in every day. I have been on many of the best known TV talk shows.

I could talk about being an alcoholic in my sleep by now. I think I do. I don't mind.

A lot of people think those commercials have made me rich. They have not. I would have done them for nothing. I did the first one for scale. I think I made less than $1,100 out of it. I think I made about the same for the others. I get no residuals for them.

Now I am getting more than personal satisfaction out of my work for Raleigh Hills. It soon became practically a full-time job. Soon I was traveling continually as their spokesperson. It reached the point where Lee thought I should be paid for my services. Advanced Health Systems thought so, too. I wouldn't ask, but Lee did. He worked out an arrangement with Herb Pratt that gives me a comfortable monthly consultant's fee.

Some of the commercials have been shot in a studio, some in our home. One was shot outdoors at someone else's home and garden in a beautiful setting in Nichols Canyon in the Hollywood Hills. Shooting outdoors poses special problems of light and sound. The light has to be right. You expect some shots to be interrupted by the sound of airplanes overhead. We were allowed to block off a road that ran nearby so the roar of motorcycles wouldn't interfere with us.

We set up by a babbling brook and started to shoot. Believe it or not, the brook babbled too loudly. They set up enormous slabs of foam between us and the brook to muffle the babbling. When we started to shoot again, there came this sharp, shrieking sound. It turned out to be the noise of power saws from over the hill where trees were being cut down. Someone went to ask for a 15-minute break while we shot some footage. The workmen agreed, but by then the sun had shifted and the technicians had to shift their reflectors.

We started to shoot again and there came this incredible pounding. It turned out to be jackhammers from around the bend where they were building some condominiums. Soon we were waiting for breaks in the noise around us so we could rush in some shots. The world was moving, the sun's position was moving, and we were moving reflectors. The road had to be reopened, and traffic noise started up. Rush hour came, then sunset.

We got our commercial, but it took us ten hours to get one good minute.

Some of the interviews have been funny. I arrived for a newspaper interview in San Diego with a busted crown on one tooth. They sent for a dentist to repair it before they took pictures. The dentist came to my hotel room and seemed thrilled to be treating My Little Margie. While he worked on me, the reporter did the interview. I didn't realize it, but the photographer took pictures at the same time. They ran a shot of me bent back in a chair, my mouth wide open, while the dentist had his hands in my throat.

20

I believe in God. I am not embarrassed to say that and I shouldn't
be. It is strange how so many people feel so embarrassed to speak
of something that is so important to them—all-important, really.
Lee and I are believers. And have based the way we have conducted
ourselves and our marriage on this belief.

I do not want to preach to anyone. Each one of us finds his own
way. I am more of an expert on alcoholism than I am on religion. But
this is my book and I want to put my belief into it. And I believe that
my becoming an alcoholic was sort of a religious experience for me.

Lee and I have been grateful to God for giving us each other and
our families and for giving us so much. We have thanked Him for
this. We have never blamed Him for our problems, whatever they
were. Perhaps we were being tested. With the strength He gave us, we
have been able to overcome our obstacles.

I have taught Sunday School in the past, but I have not practiced
my religion as much as Lee has more recently. He is an elder in our
church. He attends and sometimes conducts Bible study classes. He
has helped put together groups to do good in the church. He is more
active in our church than I am. But we have both tried to practice
religious principles in our lives. The spiritual side always has been
important to our marriage.

It was Lee who suggested to me that God had a mission for me: to
help other alcoholics. I believe God guided me to Raleigh Hills. Of

course He guided me to the other hospitals, too, and I realize now that those experiences were not a waste. Encountering failure gave me that much stronger a foundation on which to base success. If it had been easy to overcome my problem, it would have been hard to know what it was like for others.

I used to think I might be a nuisance to the staff at the hospital, but they welcome me and the other graduates. Since we've been through it, too, we speak the language of the patients. I used to wonder what to say whenever I spoke about the hospital and its system of treatment because I am not a trained speaker, but I was told that if I spoke of my experiences I couldn't go wrong.

Thad Eckman told me I had shown an insight into people and their problems that few have. That flattered me. I want it to be true. I want to get through to these people. They tell me I do. I hug them all, whether they want it or not. Here comes the hugger, they say.

Every now and then I get brought sharply back to reality by an encounter there.

I was explaining to one man how happy I was that I had had influence in getting him to the hospital where he could get help. "Lady," he said, "I ain't doing it for you; I'm doing it for me."

Lee

Gale may say it didn't take a lot of courage to admit she was an alcoholic and admit it publicly, to go through all those places in an effort to get help, and to get through the problem and to the point where she could help others, but it sure did; it took more courage than I would have had.

We had a very hard time. I was suffering right with her, but not in the way she was. There was no way I could have gotten her to seek help if she hadn't wanted to. I remember the way she clung to me and begged me not to leave her at Cedars Sinai, but she had agreed to go, and I had been warned she might try to back out.

That walk I took away from her was the hardest I've ever taken in my life. I heard her cries; I can still hear them. I love her and I would have taken her place if I could have. I went to my son's house and wept, but for her, not for me. It was typical of her to be worried about me and to call to tell me it was all right.

It wasn't all right for a long time, but there was no way I was going to leave her or give up on her. For me, marriage is for life. I knew God would answer our prayers. God comes first in my life, but Gale is a close second. My kids come pretty high, but our family started with Gale. I may act like the big boss at times, but Gale can cut me down to size pretty fast.

When we went into counseling and Phil told me I was dominating him and didn't want him to live his own life because I wanted to live it for him, it hurt more than I can say. But I tried to learn from it. I saw his point of view and he saw mine. We made changes in our ways and got to know each other better because of it.

Gale and I have had a great marriage because we try to see each other's point of view and aren't afraid to cut each other down to size when necessary. We've tried to treat the kids with the same consideration, and I think we've come out of it with great kids. As much as I tried to be the boss, they wouldn't let me.

We've tried to keep a sense of humor in our life because we don't want to take ourselves too seriously. Gale is mainly responsible for that; she has a great way of making light of heavy things.

She doesn't know the power she has over people. They honk their horns and wave to her when she's on the road. They stop her in the street and in stores. Some may not remember, but to many she's still Margie.

She was marvelous as Margie. And as Susanna. She was good in bad movies. And great in good plays. She's a wonderful actress, singer, and dancer. I just love to watch her work. It sends shivers down my spine.

She's proud of her performances, but not as proud as we are of her. She doesn't know how much her performances meant to her family and friends. Our parents, all gone now, were tremendously proud of her. Our kids are proud of her. I'm proud of her.

I am sorry I spoiled her recording career. I was the heavy; there's no doubt about it. I was seeing things that weren't there. I saw what an exciting fellow Randy Wood was and how much time they were spending together and I was afraid I might lose her or that what I had with her would be spoiled. It was like the time I asked her to quit making movies because *I* wasn't.

She doesn't ask much for herself. And I don't think she's ever received the recognition she deserves.

She was the subject of a Ralph Edwards "This Is Your Life" when she was at the peak of her career. That was something. I tricked her into the studio. Her mother was there and her old teachers and all sorts of people.

During her troubled time, I prayed for recognition for her in hopes it would boost her morale. Sure enough, out of nowhere, the Pacific Pioneer Broadcasters staged a tribute to her in 1977. It was attended by some of the greatest stars of yesterday and today.

I'm more proud of her for overcoming alcoholism than of anything else she's done. I had a lot of lonely nights during the ordeal, but she fills my life again now. I knew when I brought her back from Raleigh Hills that the ordeal was really over—that God had answered our prayers.

I've made a pretty good career in life insurance. I've been with Massachusetts Mutual since 1949. I became a district manager and opened my own office seven years later. Four of us went in together, bought a burned-out supermarket for $105,000, and remodeled it into an office building, each taking space in it.

In 1959, I was appointed a general agent for Mass Mutual, and I've recruited and trained dozens of full-time career life insurance agents since. Our agency now has over half a billion dollars of life insurance in force. I'm very proud of my associates, and of what we together have built.

Insurance may not be as glamorous as acting, but it's honest work and helpful to others. My income is based on the premium volume our agents sell each year. We expect to do a hundred million dollars' worth of volume this year, with a million and a half of premium. It is a big agency.

Just as Gale feels I have been helpful to her career, I know she has been a big asset to mine. When the time comes to turn the agency over to my successor, we will do it together—and with a great deal of pride.

Gale and I together now face an exciting future: working to help alcoholics.

21

Now that I've gotten back my good health, I feel great, better than I've felt in years. Lee has had physical problems, too, but he's in better health now than ever.

I was doing a dinner theater play in New Orleans and drinking in 1976 when he had a stroke. He was concerned about me and practically commuting between California and Louisiana when it happened.

He'd rent a car when he was in and drive me to dinner and then take me to the theater every night. He'd always stay to see the show no matter how many times he'd seen it before.

This one night, though, he said he had a little indigestion and asked if I minded if he just went back to the apartment until it was time to pick me up. I said that was fine, of course.

We were on one of those round stages, and I had to make a lot of costume changes and a lot of quick exits and entrances during brief blackouts. After I had played to the lights for a while, I couldn't see anything in the dark, so they assigned someone to me to help me off and on.

Near the end of the show my helper wasn't there and I had to feel my way off myself. It turned out he'd been with Lee and he came to tell me Lee had been rushed to the hospital.

It seems that Lee had taken some Alka Seltzer back at the apartment when he decided that exercise was what he needed, and he was doing situps with his feet on the couch when he was stricken.

Suddenly, his left side was paralyzed. He couldn't get up at first. He pulled himself up with his right arm and fell on the coffee table, breaking it.

Somehow, he got up again and dragged himself out the door, down the hall, into the elevator, and down to the garage. A security guard noticed that something was wrong with him, but Lee insisted he could manage and told him not to call the theater and disturb me.

He got the car started and somehow steered it to the theater through the narrow, winding streets in that part of town. Someone from the staff was grabbing a smoke in the alley when he saw Lee pull to a stop. He realized something was wrong and called Rick, my stage helper.

Rick got Lee into the passenger's seat and drove him to a nearby hospital, which luckily happened to be a fine one—the Ochsner Hospital.

I hurried there. A nurse told me what they thought was wrong, and I rushed to his room. It was the first time I'd ever seen him look frightened.

He said, "Honey, I've had a stroke."

I said, "No, no, you're only hyperventilating."

He said, "No, it's a stroke."

I said, "The nurse said it was hyperventilation."

He said, "I'm sorry, it's a stroke."

I was getting annoyed with him. "Why are you so negative?" I asked. He said, "At first I thought I was having a heart attack, but now I know it's a stroke. I can't move my left side. I'm sorry, but I'm sure I'm right."

He was. They decided before long that it was a stroke and told me so. It scared the dickens out of me. I was relieved that he was alive, but I worried about what damage had been done.

He was all right, though. I finished my run in the play while he finished his stay. The doctors decided there would be no aftereffects and he would be as well as he had been before once he regained his strength.

When he got home, he dragged his left leg for a while, but he has regained full use of it. It was several weeks before he was back to work, however.

He tried to slow down, but it was difficult for him to do, and soon he was pushing himself as hard as ever. The scare didn't scare him enough.

Just before Christmas, 1978, when he was carrying an armful of Christmas presents, he tripped on a curbing and fell and broke his hip. He was in the hospital for a week. He has a high tolerance for pain, but I knew he was really hurting.

He's a dictatorial patient. He expects hot-and-cold running wife. He ran me ragged.

We had one of those weekends when I went to Raleigh Hills while he went to Monarch Bay. But his sister and her family were coming out for dinner on Sunday, so I joined him at the beach house early Sunday.

Lee's not the kind to complain much, so when he told me he was having chest pains I was concerned. I wanted him to go right to a doctor, but he insisted it was indigestion and was determined not to spoil the dinner. He almost spoiled a lot of dinners.

He got through the meal, but I could see he was uncomfortable. I told him he was crazy, and he promised he'd see the doctor on Monday. He had promised to take his sister's family to Disneyland on Monday and was determined to do that first.

Sunday night we gave our sister's family our house and went to stay the night at Susie's and Joe's smaller house nearby. Lee was uncomfortable and called his doctor, Meyer Shear, but only to make an appointment for the next day. He refused to regard it as an emergency.

He did drive his sister's family to Disneyland, but he didn't stay. Instead he went to see the doctor. He telephoned from the doctor's office to tell me he'd had an EKG, which was negative, but the darn doctor was so fussy he wanted to put him in the hospital under observation.

You hate play-it-safe doctors when it turns out you're all right, but you love them when it pays off.

We were supposed to have dinner Monday night in Beverly Hills with our friends Bob and Dorothy Wood, who had also invited Charlie Schaaff and his new wife, Ruth. (Charlie, before his retirement, had been the president of Mass Mutual; it was he who had appointed Lee a general agent.) Lee insisted he felt better and could make it to the dinner party and didn't have to go to the hospital. I was furious with him.

Dr. Shear told Lee to go at his own risk, so of course he elected to come along. During dinner the pain returned; we could see he was having a hard time.

This time I took over. I sent him to the bedroom, explained to the other guests what was happening, and called Paul, who lived nearby, to drive us to the hospital. I didn't trust myself to drive. Paul helped Lee into the car and we got to the hospital faster than an ambulance could have taken us.

It turned out Lee was having a heart attack. You do not necessarily keel over unconscious with a heart attack. There are many different kinds. Each has its dangers. Each can kill. If you can get through the first one, you may never have a second, but the first one frequently kills.

The stroke Lee had suffered had been a warning. It may have been in a way a forerunner of the heart attack, because it indicated he was having arterial trouble in that the blood was having difficulty getting through to his brain and heart.

They took him to intensive care. When I went to see him, the first thing he said to me was, "Honey, I'm so glad I'm a Christian." If I was scared before, that scared me even more. I told him, "You're not going to die." But I wasn't so sure.

I thought about that saying of Emerson's, "Attitudes are more important than facts," and put it into play under fire. Disregarding the danger of Lee's condition, I acted as if he were perfectly fine and in no real peril.

I left to pray for him.

The next day when I went to Lee he was still there and I said, "Thank you, God, for my darling's heart attack." My darling looked at me like I was crazy. I had to laugh. I hadn't planned it. It had just popped into my head. I was praising God for the problem, which reinforced my feeling that everything God does is to a purpose. This had strengthened my faith.

During Lee's stay in the hospital, we came closer together than ever before. We had done and were doing for each other.

I feel that the love Lee and I can give each other now is similar to the love we give God. It is love given without question; giving without asking anything in return.

I believe there is life after death, but I don't attempt to visualize it. I'm not sure that I will see my mother, my brother and sisters, my loved ones, but I'd like to think I'd be reunited with them and with Lee.

I can't bring myself to believe in hell and eternal damnation. I don't think God is vengeful; I believe we were given the capacity to do right on earth, but should do it freely, not for fear of any punishment.

I do not know all the reasons we were put on earth, but I believe now that one reason is to do for others—as Lee and I have tried to do for one another, and for our children and parents, and for others.

As this is written, my brother Brack is battling a serious illness. He has been dealing with it better than I have. I have always felt close to him. I guess I pray for others, not for myself. I am praying for Brack now. I have prayed many times for Lee.

With treatment, Lee improved rapidly. They took tests and determined that there was no need for heart surgery. However, some time after he was sent home, he began to feel bad again. They took new tests and decided that he needed surgery after all. They had been looking for the vascular trouble near his heart, but found it in his neck. There were blockages in his carotid arteries. So he had neck surgery less than a year ago. It was successful, and he was soon feeling better than he had felt in many years.

Lee does not smoke or drink, but boy how he watches his diet! He read about the Pritikin health plan and insisted we enroll at the Pritikin Institute in Santa Monica for a four-week stay. I was supposed to be his companion, but I was crummy company. I do not enjoy measuring out fish and chicken and stuff like that to the ounce. I could not live long on raw fruit and vegetables.

You know what "jicama" is? It's pronounced "hick-ah-mah" and it's nature's food. Not mine. Lee eats it all the time. He offers some to everyone who comes by.

I am sure Pritikin's is a very healthful diet, especially for people with heart problems. So I had to learn to prepare it. But I wonder why so many good things in life are bad for us.

They also emphasize exercise. At Pritikin's, we did aerobic dancing. It was lovely—like doing the Charleston in place. I love dancing, unless they call it exercise.

Lee is supposed to walk briskly every day to get the blood pumping through his system. He is walking five miles every day. He is very good about it. He would be. The problem was he wanted me to walk with him. He has long legs and I have short ones. I can't keep up with him. I don't want to. So I gave him a Treadmill; two people can't get on it.

We feel we are lucky to have each other. But, speaking about my marriage in public recently, I said, "We never have considered divorce. Murder, yes, but not divorce." I can kid because we have been so lucky to have a marriage that has lasted so long, that has outlasted so many problems.

I feel we have been lucky with our children, too. They are all on their own now and doing very well. All are married and all but the youngest have children. Each has made a different life for himself or herself. We feel fortunate, too, in all the in-laws we have gained; it was no struggle to love them.

Lee would have liked his sons to follow in his footsteps, into life insurance. He considers it work that feeds you spiritually as well as financially. He believes you do well for others as well as for yourself. He considers it a much more stable career than show business. But he never pushed his children into it. And only one, Paul, went into it.

None of them ever wanted to be in show business. I never pushed any of them into it. But one—Phil—has gone into it. He studied economics at the University of Southern California. Then, he took a $25,000 settlement from that auto accident and went to study at the Neighborhood Playhouse in New York. Diane Keaton was in his class. Phil had worked with me on the road in *Wildcat* at one time. Now he went on the road with the veteran actor Sam Levene, in *The Impossible Years*. However, although he has the ability and looks for it, he really isn't turned on by acting. His interest lies more in production.

He came home to lie around awhile, however, thinking things through, but annoying Lee. Lee wanted his son to get going. After counseling, they got together, and Phil got his act together.

His college roommate had been Dwight Chapin, Richard Nixon's appointments secretary. Through Dwight, Phil applied for and got a job with the U.S. Information Agency, moving to Washington. When Nixon resigned, everyone resigned. Phil returned to southern California and formed a television production partnership with Jim Irvine, part of a prominent Orange County family.

After a year and a half, Phil left to be on his own. He's been doing some great things, even though he's really just starting. He recently did a special on Liberace from Las Vegas for cable television.

Phil married a teacher, Jan. They have two daughters, Alexis and Tristan, and they live in Orange County, in El Toro, near our beach house.

Peter was not interested in being a student. He always preferred a physical life. He liked the outdoors, not the indoors. This concerned Lee, but he gave our son all the help he could. Peter served with the Marines in Vietnam, under fire. We worried dreadfully about him, but he came home safely.

He went into business with Lee for a while, but realized soon that he still wanted an outdoor life. So he went into the Parks Department, electing to serve as a forest ranger in Alaska. He did wild, dangerous work for some years, but felt he was away from his wife and daughters too much and now is serving as a firefighter in Juneau. This may be equally dangerous, but requires less travel.

He and his Ginny have two daughters, also—Kimberly and Karri. I don't think they spell too well. We don't see them as much as we'd like. They are not exactly next door. Advanced Health Systems flew them in to be with us at Susie's wedding in June of 1980, as a gift to me, and I was thrilled.

Susie married a fine fellow named Joe Harrigan, who is an executive with Procter & Gamble. For a while they lived in Orange County, but he was transferred to Phoenix last year. They have a new house and a new boat. The boat looks funny on the desert. Actually, there are a lot of lakes there.

However, they also are not exactly next door. We did spend some time with them at Christmas. And also this summer. Those were wonderful visits.

Susie also went to USC and majored in French. I'm sure it comes in handy with all the French-speaking people in Phoenix.

Paul followed Lee into insurance, but with Pacific Mutual, which I'm sure is a nice little company. I say that in jest. Paul majored in business at USC and took management training under Lee with Mass Mutual before deserting to the other company to be on his own. He doesn't like to sell, but his father says he is an excellent administrator.

I now have divided loyalties. If Mass Mutual ever played Pacific Mutual in football, I don't know which I'd root for.

Paul is married to a lovely girl named Gail—who *obviously* can't spell—and they have come through with a son, Ryan Peter. They live in Reseda, right here in the Valley; we are happy to have them so close.

I'd like to have all of our kids close to us, but I think it's good for them, once they are grown and with families of their own, to be on their own. We never wanted to live their lives for them. We knew the mistakes we'd made and we didn't want them to make the same ones. I'm sure most parents feel the same way.

We did try to give them good guidance. We guided them to God. We live by the golden rule and such and tried to teach them to be fair with everybody and honest in everything. To give of themselves, to give to others. I think we succeeded.

We tried to set good examples for them. Obviously, we weren't always able to do so. I certainly wasn't. My drinking was a bad example. While I was drinking, I neglected them. But I hope that by battling to overcome this obstacle, by overcoming it, and by using what I learned from it to help others, I have since set a good example.

I love my work, show business. I had to live my own life. I hope my children understand this. As much as I could, I took them on my sets, and they loved it. Lee often took them to his office, too.

We have had vacation homes and have taken many vacation trips together. We were always with them as much as we could be.

We always made it clear we would be there for them whenever they needed us. We always were. We like to think that the quality of the time we spent with them made up for any lack of quantity. And there were long periods of time when I was not working a lot when I spent a lot of time with them.

I feel close to them, and I know Lee does, too. We have always given them a lot of love, and we have a lot of love to give.

Like husbands and wives, parents and children often have problems relating to one another, but if you work at it, get help with it, and stay with it, you can work it out.

As the children of a celebrity, ours were pulled this way and that at times, but they never permitted themselves to be pulled out of shape. They handled the problem well and grew up normally.

Of course I like to think they are the best, and special, but what mother doesn't? Lee and I think they are good kids and we like to think we have given them a lot of good things, things that matter.

Kids? The oldest, Phil, is thirty-eight. Peter is thirty-five, Paul thirty-four. Susie is twenty-four. But they will always be our kids.

Phil

No matter how hard you try to downplay the identity of a famous parent in the family, the word gets out, and part of your identity becomes mixed with that well-known parent's. As a youngster I think the thing that bothered me most was the thought that if my mother was highly valued by others, but did not spend time with me, then I must not be highly valued by her.

When we were children, our parents talked to us about how our mother was mom at home, and not a star, and how important it was to keep this in perspective. And I think we tried to do this, although it wasn't easy. I remember very well all the fan magazine photo sessions we had to endure as her children. We had to dress up in costumes and assume awkward poses. I recall feeling like a stage prop, an ornament to Mom's career. Even at a very young age I knew those photographers weren't there because they wanted to feature pictures of Phillip Bonnell in their magazines. I finally came to the point where I never told a new friend that my mother was Gale Storm. In fact, after I was graduated from college and moved to New York City, people I would come to know well never suspected that Mom wasn't a housewife. It's not that I was ashamed of Mother. It was that I had to learn to believe in myself to the point where I knew I was of real value as Phillip Bonnell, not just as Gale Storm's son. When friends or acquaintances eventually discovered who Mother was, they quite naturally asked, "Why didn't you tell me?" I lamely fell back on, "You didn't ask." I still don't make a point of bringing up my maternal roots when I meet someone. But my feelings about Mom and myself have come around 180 degrees. Today, I'm damned proud to have come from that kind of quality stock.

There are good memories as well. . . . I remember her coming into our bedroom when she'd get home at night and singing us lullabies in that sweet voice of hers. One song was "Alice Blue Gown." Another was "If You Should Go to Venice."

I remember her taking us to the studio so we could romp around the unused sets. I remember their taking us on vacations and I remember saying the same things to them that our kids now say—"How much farther do we have to go . . . when will we get there?" I know that for all the time she had to be away from us, she wanted very much for us to feel like a family.

Looking back, I think if Mom had become an attorney or a surgeon instead of an actress she would have been away just as much. She is an intelligent woman who, with proper education, could very well have followed a different career. But Mom had a God-given ability and she used it.

What happened in Mom's and Dad's marriage was that her early success caused Dad to persuade her to relinquish authority to him. He gave the punishments, though they were rare. If one of us was reprimanded in school, he'd deal with it.

But there was a very fundamental difference in their expectations of and attitudes toward us. Dad set the goals and established the priorities in my life. They were deceptively simple—succeed, follow him into the life insurance business, and eventually assume his mantle of leadership. These are not unusual demands to be made upon a son by his father, but Dad pressed them with exceptional vigor. I was on the football team and captain of the swim team in high school. I was senior class president. I was king of the senior prom. I was Chief Justice of The Men's Judicial at the University of Southern California. Dad even tried to choose my college major for me, business. I fooled him on that one, however, and talked him into economics, which was placed in the School of Letters, Arts and Sciences instead of the School of Business. This allowed me numerous electives (e.g., history, literature, political science, international relations, etc.) that I never could have taken as a business major. I cite these instances not to criticize Dad but to give you an idea of the impact he had on our lives and the enormous degree of power Mother gave up in our family decision-making process. Dad is a compassionate, giving and patient man, but he also has one strong ego. He never liked being addressed as Mr. Storm.

Ironically, Mom wanted my love and acceptance as much as I wanted hers. With Mom, there were never any strings attached. Dad too wanted my love and acceptance, but he also wanted imitation, the sincerest form of flattery. Dad specialized in strings.

Please keep in mind that I'm talking about a long growing process—both for Dad and for myself—and we've both grown up. Our relationship now is one of great love and mutual respect. I seek his advice and he seeks mine. But now there is one big difference. I also seek Mom's counsel and she seeks mine. Growing up wasn't easy, but it sure as hell wasn't boring.

We were more aware of Mom's drinking than she realizes. It was rarely talked about, but we knew. We spoke of it only in whispers in safe places; the silence was a family conspiracy.

Mother went through a prolonged hell to overcome her alcoholism. It took incredible courage and a great deal of faith. It took guts to go public so she could help others. I'm tremendously proud of her and what she has accomplished.

I love the lady.

She's a class act.

Pete

I was conscious of being the child of a celebrity. The kids in school knew. Wherever we went she was recognized. We had to pose for a lot of publicity pictures when I'd rather have been out fooling around. I didn't like it, but I thought that if my mother was important, being her son made me important.

But my parents took pains to point out to us that we were no better, no worse than anyone else, that we would be whatever we made of ourselves. They gave us a good perspective on life.

We never went out to dinner that someone didn't ask her for an autograph. If it bothered us, it didn't bother her. We might have said something about people being inconsiderate of our privacy, but I never heard her make a derogatory remark. She felt that her fans cared about her, so she cared about them. She was always as gracious as she could be. I learned from that.

When I got into that incident later, when the other guys broke into the school, I was only charged with having an open container of beer in my vehicle, but more was made of me than of them; more was made of it than should have been. It bothered me, but it bothered Dad more. He was infuriated. It went against his sense of fair play.

I disappointed Dad with the grades I got in school—I'm the least scholarly member of our family—but he was able to resign himself to this. He got me tutors; he did what he could do; he stressed that I had other strengths; and he tried to keep my confidence up.

A lot of his life has been dedicated to insurance, and there is nothing he would have liked better than for his sons to go into it with him. He was thrilled when I came out of the Marine Corps, did better in college, and showed some interest in insurance.

But when I went another way, toward an outdoors life, he accepted it. He still says, "Pete, you had what it takes; you could've been a salesman; you could've made it big." But he's risen above it; he's given my wife and me all the support we could want.

We all have our faults, but to me my dad comes as close to being a man of good reason and great integrity as anyone I've ever known. I respect him greatly and try to emulate him. If you had to put someone on the bench to be a judge, he'd be the one I'd like to see there.

Maybe our parents weren't with us as much as they might have been, but when they were with us they must have done something right, because I feel I've been given a great set of values to live my life by, and I don't know where else it could have come from. I really feel a lot of love and a lot of warmth toward them both. They were busy, but we spent time together as a family. Mom took us and sometimes our friends to the Hal Roach studios on Saturdays, and we'd spend the whole day there and have a great time. She was well liked there, so we were treated well. The makeup man would put scars on us, and we'd run through the vacant sets getting into mischief. She was always worried about where we were. One time we crawled into the rafters of an old building, got stuck, and had to be rescued by the fire department.

We got to play on the old Laurel and Hardy and Little Rascals sets. We got to see them shoot Mom's shows. We got a great appreciation of how difficult it all was. But I didn't like to watch her shows. One I did like was the "Susanna" show with my little sister in it when she was a baby.

Mom was working six days a week, so I didn't get to see her much. I remember it would still be dark when she got up to drive herself to work, and it was late at night when she came back. She was under a lot of pressure. And she had terrible back problems. They wanted her to go on working, so she did. I can remember one night my dad had to carry her into the house from the car because she was in such pain she was screaming.

I also remember Dad picking her up off the couch at night and carrying her to bed because she had passed out.

I think different things caused her to turn to drink. I didn't like it because I was afraid I'd bring some friends home and be embarrassed by her, but it never really happened, though many of them knew.

Maybe the others didn't talk about it, but I talked to her about it. This was when I came out of the Marines. She was sad, a celebrity sitting around with nothing to do. She didn't like herself then. She wanted to change. But it was hard.

It was a long, hard battle; and, to tell the truth, I figured she'd kill herself before she ever cured herself. I was surprised she was able to overcome her problems. I'm as proud of her as I can be.

I think it's great that it's gotten her some attention again and given her something to do which makes her feel useful. I think she's the answer to many people's prayers. I don't go out of my way to tell people my mom is the actress, but I tell them she's an alcoholic and she's overcome it.

I'd stand up alongside her anytime and tell people, "This is my mom and she's an alcoholic and she's helping others overcome it and I'm as proud of her as I can be."

Paul

My mother may not have been around that much when I was growing up, but I don't remember being bothered by it. Whenever I needed her, she was there.

Going to the studio was a real treat because everyone treated us like little princes. ZaSu Pitts was especially nice, and somehow always had doughnuts for us in her dressing room.

The makeup men would put gruesome scars and black eyes on us. We'd get guns and swords out of the prop department and then battle from deck to deck on fake ships. It was a super playground for us, and an ego trip, too. We got a vicarious thrill out of our mom's glamor.

There was no way to escape it, anyway. Every time you got into a new group or a new school everyone knew about it some way. I always worried about if they were interested in me for me or because of my mother.

On the other hand, there was something seductive about feeling that because she was unique and special, you were unique and special. It was hard not to feel like you were royalty.

She and Dad didn't want us to feel this way and did try to bring us up in normal circumstances. Some of my friends had money, but none were the children of famous actors. I tried to look on her as my mom, not as an actress.

She's a good person. I can't forget that when fans came up to her to ask for an autograph, she'd always ask them their names so she could personalize it, and she'd always chat with them and be nice to them.

People always did make a big deal over her. Somehow we were never able to develop that bonding I see in other sons and mothers who are home all the time, who make their sandwiches and send them off to school. It's too bad because we'd both have liked it.

My father ran our family. He was no stage-door husband waiting in the wings for his wife. He actively controlled her career. He was a very powerful catalyst in all our lives. And he was always fair with us. Both of them were. Neither had a hair-trigger temper or was vindictive.

When we had to be punished, it was Dad's duty. If you had been told not to do something and you did it, you knew you had to pay a

159

price for it. You might get a spanking. But very ritualistic. Over the counter in the bathroom. Very structured. Non-terrorizing.

They both tried to be model parents. Dad took time off from work to attend my high school swim meets. Whatever we wanted to do, they wanted it for us.

He wanted all of us to go into insurance. But all he did was say it was a great opportunity for us and ask why didn't we take a look at it. We all did. That I was the one who went into it may be more because I didn't know what I wanted to do and less that the others didn't like it. They eventually found other things they wanted to do.

I always saw Dad as strong, dynamic, and attractive. I didn't realize it, but I guess I always wanted to be like him. He was a role model for me. But I went to another insurance company because I had to get out on my own.

He is the sort of person who likes to be needed, who likes people to come to him for help, who likes to help. I admired this in him, but it is easy to become too dependent on him. He will do too much for you if you let him.

He and my mother have lived their lives on very strong religious principles. We were taken to church regularly. We were asked to live by the golden rule. It was good for us, no doubt about it.

Maybe it was because I was younger, but I don't remember my mother drinking too much until the 1970s. It bothered me, but I wasn't around it that much. I knew she'd had bad back problems and I figured that led to drinking.

Finally, at Dad's prompting, she started looking for help, but after she'd been to two or three places without getting any better, I figured she was just indulging Dad. He was giving her the best help money could buy, and she was still drinking. I figured if professionals couldn't help her, she'd kill herself in time.

We used to kid that we were keeping the local liquor store in business. I didn't think of my mom as being strong-willed enough to kick her habit. But then I never thought she'd be able to stop smoking, and I was surprised and impressed when she did. And I was even more surprised and impressed when she stopped drinking. It was something special, really. I think when she found out it was a disease and it was not totally her fault it gave her the courage to get through it. It was either kill yourself or get your act together.

I'm sorry she had to suffer so, but I'm glad she's getting so much out of it now. She has a sense of duty, and it's good for her to be able to help others. I'm pleased she's turned such a negative thing into such a positive one.

I don't think any of us feel any embarrassment over her admission of alcoholism, and I think it was best that she went public so she could help others.

Susie

When I was very young Mom wasn't working as much as I guess she had been. When I was in the third grade or so, she decided to do a play away from home. I didn't want her to go because I thought I couldn't live without her. She was away six weeks or so and I found I could. I also found a feeling of independence that kept me from being as close to her as she wanted me to be. She only went away three or four times a year, but I depended on my feeling of independence. I always found fault with her. I feel bad about it now. She didn't deserve it.

Unlike my brothers, I went to a private school, and many of my friends were the children of actors and actresses. None of us wanted to be different from other children, but we were. Our parents gave us our importance. But my parents tried not to make it important. I remember seeing reruns of my mother's television shows and thinking it was no big deal. But she was proud of her performances. And my father was proud of her. He took me to Texas and other places at times to see her in the theater. She looked like a different person to me when she was up there. As an actress, she was really good.

All along, my father was the strong one, the one we'd turn to for advice, the one who did the disciplining. I don't know if that was true for my brothers. I came so long after them that I was practically raised as an only child. By the time I was a teen-ager, they had left home.

They were all gone when my mother's drinking really became a problem. Well, we all have our problems; I see that now. I used to say my mother was my problem. I see now that it wasn't true. I was my own problem.

I wish I could have helped her more. She suffered so. But I couldn't understand why she couldn't just stop. When I wanted her to stop smoking, she did. I wanted her to stop drinking, but she didn't.

I was going with the man I later married, and his mother took me to an Al-Anon meeting. That's the family branch of Alcoholics Anonymous. She had someone in her family who was an alcoholic. She helped me, because going there made me see how hard it was to stop, how much suffering alcoholics go through. It made me sympathetic to my mother's problem. It made me appreciate it when she overcame it. For a while, I was waiting for something to go wrong. She'd trip or something and I'd think she was drinking again. It took a while for me to be comfortable with her and her sobriety. I'm really proud of how she's using it to benefit others.

We've talked a lot lately. She made me see how I was finding fault with her unfairly. She never found fault with me. She was always fair to me. There is no perfect mother. I know that now. The one I have is good enough for me. We're closer now than we've ever been.

Oh, we live far apart, but closeness isn't a matter of miles. My husband, Joe, and I visited them at Christmastime. My husband and I had an argument over a family matter. He walked out, which he'd never done before. I was hysterical. Mom came to me and calmed me down. She was wonderful.

I know now that she was always there when I needed her, and always will be. My dad, too. I know now they gave us great guidance. Not only in obvious ways like taking us to church, but in more subtle ways, too.

I think all parents and children have problems. I think it's how we work out our problems that lets us make something of our lives. It's important to have had a family life that gives you those things you need in order to live well. And I think I've had that.

22

I have said repeatedly that my family comes first with me. In my heart, it always did. I think we have consistently tried to do right by one another.

Lee and I always have felt that the spiritual side was the most important part of our lives. I don't think there's a contradiction there. I think one way we express our love for God is by loving others.

To me, giving to others and doing for others is a religious experience.

I believe it was part of God's plan that I experience alcoholism so I could help alcoholics. And Lee has always wanted to help others who needed help.

The publisher of this book is Bobbs-Merrill. Recently, while going through some things back home after his father's death, Lee found his first reader. His First Reader! Looking at it, he laughed and showed it to me. The publisher was Bobbs-Merrill. The publisher of his first book and his last. This is his book as much as it is mine. It is his life as much as it is mine.

The first book was published in 1908. I hope the company will yet be in business a while longer. The company was founded in Indianapolis. Lee is from South Bend.

I have come to the conclusion that Jesus Christ put his teachings into parables because He didn't want to just say Do this or Don't do that; he wanted us human beings to consider what He had to say and to work things out for ourselves.

163

I have tried to do this, and I am still trying.

Lee is my life. But my children are my life, too. And my grandchildren. And show business is my life. And my God is my life. And practicing God's work. And not drinking. In a way, we all live many lives. And I think I have a lot of life yet to live.

I ain't down *yet*.

Hi. I'm Gale Storm and I am celebrating a birthday. It is two years since I was treated for alcoholism at Raleigh Hills Hospital. Years of sobriety, happiness, and freedom from craving alcohol. I have received continued reinforcement, and today I share my sobriety with many Raleigh Hills graduates. With God's help and our combined strength, we lead happy, productive lives. If alcohol is a problem in your life, Raleigh Hills can help.

Television commercial,
early 1981